Briard

Seasons

Njungwa Susankembling Nkola

 New Generation Publishing

Njungwa Susankembling Nkola is a Cameroonian. She is the third of eight girls. She was born in her native town of Fontem in the south western region of The Cameroon in 1978, and attended primary school in a neighbouring town, Mamfe, later returning to her native Town to attend secondary school. *Bridges - Hard Seasons* is her first piece of writing. Still a student at the Manchester Metropolitan University, she lives in Manchester, England, with her husband and children.

Dedication

'O Lord my God, when I in awesome wonder
consider all the worlds thy hands have made.'
Carl G. Boberg (1885)

Dedication

Daddy, my dear Daddy! I received a phone call at 2.35 in the morning. All I heard was screaming, and scream I did too! I was told you could no longer speak, that your sweet smile was gone with the wind. I planned to thank you in the morning for all the amazing lessons in life that you passed on to me, and your unending struggle to help me stand on higher ground.

I longed for a special moment with you - I wanted to make it a special occasion because I was truly grateful. But I wasted too much time, and I guess even hours sometime became ages, and some things never come.

I miss you, Daddy. I know there is no point writing this now, but my heart tells me you might read this someday. Daddy, I have written my first novel, and I want to say thank you.

Acknowledgments

My mother, my African queen, my channel to this Earth, with love I salute you.

My husband (Leke Aka) and children: I see you all beaming with pride, and you do not have to say anything. But I sincerely appreciate the time and space you gave me so that now I might be called an Author. You all complete my world.

I sometimes think it would be better for me to be one of the birds in the sky or the fishes in the sea; I love freedom, the freedom which can make me queen of the heavens and the oceans. You all make me see differently: Nven Pruddy Imafu Nkola, Atabong Debby Nkola, Jacky Shetu, Asong Juliet Nkola, Fualefeh Irene Njuangang Nkola, Ajab Regina Nkola and Abangma Cecil Tabot. My darling sisters, you helped me change my view, and I love you all so much.

Some say I am not famous, but I say wait until you see who my friends are: Adeline Longla Tambe, Esther Arrey Tabot Enaw, Yoba Patoutchou Edith Karine, Vera Nchana Mpafa, Bate Bridget nee Branz, Dr.Sylvia Likambe Forchap, Constance Mandi, Adeline Kien Chi and Florence Maey Mforsong.

And even my family friends make me mighty famous: Adel Njuangang, Dr Stanley Njuangang, Perry Imafu, Etengeneng Tataw and Njoh Terence Teke.

I had ten pairs of extra eyes, forty extra fingers and amazing minds shielding and directing these ideas. Their confidence in me surpasses all. Fuelefeh Irene Njuangang Nkola, Constance Mandi, Esther Arrey Tabot Enaw, Yoba Patoutchou Edith Karine, Leke Aka Oben.

We made this happen - may God bless you all mightily.

'There is no story that is not true.'
Chinua Achebe, *Things Fall Apart*

'The most beautiful people we have known are those who
have known defeat, known suffering, known struggle,
known loss, and have found their way out of those depths.'

Elisabeth Kubler-Ross

Locks and Bolts

Locks and bolts everywhere. Some of them clicked open just at the sound of your footsteps, but many had secret codes or numbers; either way the doors shut silently behind you once you went through. It was scary, very scary. She pinched herself - could she have imagined such a world? Even if she had read about it in books, it would not have changed her expectations, and she would not have imagined all this. It was as if there were invisible people watching her every move. Was it an open prison? Tiny spaces with made-to-measure chairs, *hello*'s and *hi*'s that embodied no feeling, and accompanied by fake smiles. How could you tell a foe from a friend? This land had been programmed. She swore to herself: the land was definitely programmed, including its inhabitants. John Biggs, Deborah's government solicitor, did not look at her and smile weirdly as every other person of his skin colour did, but still she was convinced beyond any doubt that the people of this land were automated.

Ah! Deborah shook her head in disbelief. Jude – who she had paid for the journey from her home and to get her into the country – was a cheat, she whispered to herself, what they called a '419' in their home country, a complete con man. "Honesty is a very expensive gift, don't expect it from cheap people." Warren Buffett was right about this. Whilst growing up she had always associated ugliness with wickedness, but her friends would say she was too judgemental. Now she was absolutely convinced that there was a strong connection between the two. Jude's face was like a piece of homemade soap. He looked just like the 'coco-soap' made by the villagers in her country - completely shapeless. When he closed his eyes he looked exactly like death.

When she had first met him she was so consumed by sorrow that his words were like water to a dying plant in the desert! A desperate woman, one can say, ready to run away, far, far away from everything she had ever known. So he was her salvation. How could someone look you in the face and tell such a blatant lie? Many people say the country Jude had brought her to, was the land of honey and fresh milk. But Deborah could certainly tell that one would have to endure the stings of the bees to get the honey, and the milk always seemed to be on the verge of turning sour.

CHAPTER 1

Brixton Underground
Station

It had been three days since Deborah followed Sami onto the bus from Brixton tube station in London. Initially Sami had made up his mind not to listen to whatever she had to say or to help her, but her persistence paid off. She tailed him all the way to where he alighted from the bus; and finally he gave up.

"Stay here and do not move an inch'', said Jude.

He reassured that he was going to get the person with whom Deborah would be living and working, as he had promised before they left Cameroon. He slipped his hand into his pocket and took out a twenty pound note, explaining that there might be a lot of traffic on his way to wherever he was going, so that if she felt hungry before his return she should buy herself something to eat. He pointed at the shops around the Brixton underground station. Then just as the money was about to touch her palm, he seized it and vanished into the crowd. After a minute or so he returned with some coins which together still made twenty pounds. As he counted it out, he explained the different coins to her. The two pound coin had the highest value, and a pound or two should be enough to purchase a packet of biscuits and a can of coke.

He told her that there were a lot of professional thieves in cities such as London. He warned her to be on her guard, as people in London stole more than rats and no one was to be trusted. She whispered yes and thanked him. He was just about to take his leave when he saw the fear on her face. He hesitated and then came closer, reassuring her that

1

he would not be gone for more than two hours. She looked up at him and motioned that she would be waiting.

She watched him walked away - slowly at first, as if he was assessing something, but then he quickened his pace and disappeared into the sea of people in front of the station. At first she felt all alone and frightened, but soon she was distracted by the activity around the station. Who would not have been?

Everything – London, the people – was new and unfamiliar to her. She had come across some busy places in her life, when she visited Lagos on her way to Kaduna to get some goods for her shop, for example, but that was nothing compared the sights that surrounded her now.

The streets in front of her were packed with hundreds and thousands of people. People and cars were jostling for space on the road. One could hear the constant squealing of brakes as the cars stopped to avoid hitting people. She cursed under her breath.

Were these people not afraid of being killed? Did they just want to die for nothing?

She thought back to the rush hour in Douala, the economic capital of her country, and asked herself if it was anything like what she was observing, and shook her head in disagreement. In Douala there were no traffic lights on most of the busy roads, so people had no option but to dodge between the cars to cross the road, and so the traffic was slower. But from where she was standing now she could see three different sets of traffic lights.

So what could be the rush?

There were also plenty of people just loitering about, but more than half were walking in a hurry. There were mothers dragging kids and at the same time pushing a pushchair - and a lot of them were pregnant. The scene could have been where motherhood had originated!

Are the women in this city always in the family way?

She later on learned that it was quite normal to find more women heavy with child in spring and summer than in winter, as that is the time when people get cosy and cuddle up to one another. Not that many people venture out in the cold, so more people indulge in extra-marital activities, the result of which is a baby boom.

One thing she did unquestionably appreciate was how organised the people in the busy crowd were. There was virtually no pushing or bumping, and almost everyone seemed to have a sense of direction: even the mums with the babies knew which way to walk. People seemed to be emerging and disappearing every minute in a smoothly synchronized way, and it occurred to her that if someone stared at the crowd for long enough, they might be convinced they were by the sea watching the waves come and go. She felt so excited surveying this mass movement of people. She thought it was magical how thousands of people could organise themselves to emerge and disappear, and she wondered at the way they managed to do it. She also noticed that there were a lot of people just sitting around or leaning against the station wall, some murmuring to themselves and some begging from Passers-by.

But there was one particular man who was neither begging nor talking to himself, and she thought he must have been insane. Who on earth would imagine that somebody might

3

share a can of beer with a dog and constantly kiss the dog on the mouth! She heard him calling the dog Daisy and sometimes Baby. Every time it moved an inch he would say, 'Come, Daisy! Come back here, Baby!'

She punched her left leg in disbelief and gazed in astonishment: 'Baby' indeed! She tried to imagine this madman and his dog in Muyuka, a small town in her home country - Baby would be seen only as the main ingredient for an excellent pot of dog meat pepper soup.

She soon got fed up of watching the masses of people going up and down by the station, and started thinking of Jude again. She wondered what he was doing or maybe where he was. Wherever he had gone, it must truly have been a good distance away;

Was he on his way back to come and get her?

Now, lying in the quietness of Sami's living room, she felt certain that Jude would never return for her. When she had seen Sami and made up her mind to follow him and seek help, she must have been waiting for more than ten hours, for it was already nightfall and she had not moved an inch, as Jude had instructed. Although she wanted to buy food and other things, she had no idea how to use the money he had given her. His desultory effort to teach her the values of the coins had failed, as she could not make out the difference. As she stood there, her head was spinning like a carousel and it was obvious that she was either waiting or searching for some one. When it finally dawned on her that she might have been abandoned, she was too saddened and weakened to shed tears or cry.

She thought to herself, "I ran away from my country barely thirty-six hours ago, believing I was going to find

4

safety and be able to make a fresh start. Now here I am, alone in the middle of nowhere." The thought of being forsaken by Jude sent a chill down her spine. She wanted to cry but she knew too well that crying never amounted to anything; she had cried so many times in her life in vain. Thoughts and questions were rushing through her mind like a wild wind: what was going to happen to her if Jude really did not return? Was she going to die?

It was getting really dark and the cold was bitter; it felt as though she was in an open freezer. She was now shivering from the cold and was frightened, too.

Would she ever see her parents and her son again?

As she thought of all the promises and reassurances that Jude had given to her parents and herself, guaranteeing her safety and promising her a much better life, she collapsed slowly by the station wall and moaned quietly.

Then she did start to cry: the betrayal was too much to bear and the thought of what to do next was unthinkable. Occasionally you encounter people who tell you how they've helped so many people in your situation and how they have been a saviour to so many others, and you just think they are good. She had been convinced that Jude was an exceptional man from all the stories he told them, and she had been so grateful to God and to Jude himself for the opportunity to escape from the torments of the Cameroon government. But now she realised that things were turning out in a completely different way.

While still in despair at the thought of the situation she was in and wondering what she was going to do next, she was distracted by a voice. It was a dark skin man, of average build and he was standing very close, talking into his telephone. She could understand the French he was speaking. She knew he might be from Africa, but certainly not from her part of Africa as his accent a little different from what she was used to. She looked up immediately, and saw that his face had a friendly expression. He finished his phone call and was fidgeting with the phone in his hands as she approached him. At first she could not find words to say, as she had not spoken to anyone since Jude left her. He realised she was having difficulties.

"Can I help you?" he asked.

After a momentary hesitation she managed to tell him that someone had asked her to wait for him that morning but had not returned for her. He looked at her sternly and said, "what has that got to do with me'?"

She said nothing and quickly took a little step back as she remembered how Jude had warned her that nobody was to be trusted. He did not reply, but immediately turned his back on her. However, something within urged her not to give up but to explain further, and so she moved closer again, but as she was about to speak once more a bus pulled up in front of them and he hopped on.

She followed him onto the bus. It was not until months later that she realised she was supposed to pay a fare, but right then she was too pre-occupied with making sure she did not lose sight of Sami, as he was her only hope. On the bus, she remained standing and holding onto one of the poles so that she could have a clear view of him. Every now and then he looked at her and shook his head as if in disbelief, but that did not bother her at all as her conviction that he could help her was getting stronger. When he got off the bus she followed suit, but again was confused about what to say.

6

She said, "Excuse me, brother - is this London?"

He turned around furiously. "Of course this is London!" he said. He continued to look at her and hissed, "And who the hell is your brother?"

She immediately explained to him that where she came from, it was polite to address somebody as brother or sister if you did not know their name, but before she could finish, he said, "Where the hell are you from?"

"Cameroon" she replied, adding that she had only arrived yesterday.

"Yesterday?"

"Yes."

"So what in God's name are you doing following me around?"

She explained to him that during the whole of the time she had been waiting near the station he had been the only person she had seen with anything like a friendly or familiar face, and the only one who spoke any language that she recognised. She told him that everyone who had gone past her had been either too serious or too busy, and they had all spoken a language that sounded like English but she had had absolutely no idea what they were saying. She was frustrated and exhausted, and he must have felt it in her voice. When she whispered desperately that she needed his help as she had nowhere to go, he just looked away from her.

He then spoke to her again to tell her he lived with his fiancée. She swore to him that she would be no trouble and she was just looking for help. He told her to follow him. However, he added that there was no guarantee she could stay with them as his fiancée would have to agree. He introduced himself formally to her as Sami, and she told him her name was Deborah.

Sami's girlfriend, Esther, was very sympathetic and nice to her – in fact, she was as much of an angel as her namesake in the Bible. Africans believe in the power of names, so children are called what their parents want them to represent. When Sami told Deborah that his girlfriend's name was Esther, she prayed. She asked the Almighty that she might find favour in her and be saved by her, just like the Jews in the Old Testament when they were saved by Queen Esther.

When they arrived at Sami's place, Esther offered her some of her clothes to wear and also made sure she was warm and comfortable. She ensured she also had enough to eat all the time. All this made her feel welcome. As she had been worried and sick at Brixton station, she had not realised how cold and tired she was. Her first night in Sami's house she slept like a baby. Esther had arranged the sofa bed for her in the living room. She was still sleeping when they returned from work the next day. When Esther found her still sleeping she was troubled she had not eaten anything, but Deborah told her she was fine. She said that she was quite used to spending a day or two without food. She heard her grumbling as she stepped out of the sitting room, saying that such a life style was not healthy as not eating regularly could wear down your system.

On the third day of her stay, when Sami returned from work he said that he would like to speak with her about something. After dinner he beckoned her to sit by his side and showed her a piece of paper with an address on. He explained to her that very early in the morning she would have to go to that address.

He explained that the place was like a refugee headquarters; called the 'Home Office', and that it belonged to the British government. He said he would have loved to keep her in his house until she found her feet, but that would not be possible. In England, anyone who needed help or was in her situation had to go to the Home Office. She felt rejection again, but he further explained that for her to stay in his house was illegal. But how was she to understand what was lawful or not when she desperately needed shelter and had lost it, just as she thought she had found it? She asked Sami what she should say to the people at the refugee headquarters. He said that she should tell them about Jude, who had brought her into the country and abandoned her. He also told her that if the people at the office needed more information, then they would ask her, and she should respond accordingly. Although she was now confused again, she thanked him gladly.

That night she could not sleep. Her mind was occupied with the last talk she had had with Sami. All night long she kept thinking of the Home Office and how she would seek help. She was not prepared for all these problems. When he was given 3.5 million Cameroon francs, Jude had promised her parents, her boyfriend Smith and herself that she would have a house and a job waiting for her at her final destination. Though she felt sorry for herself, she wondered how many desperate people might have also fallen into the hands of the likes of Jude. She looked up at the ceiling, pondering her fate and scared of what might happen to her the next day. Sami and his girlfriend had been very helpful and she was very grateful. Nonetheless, the sudden uncertainty that lay ahead of her was overwhelming. Deborah started to weep slowly again. She wept for her dear life. She thought of going back to Cameroon - but how could she do that? Even the slightest thought of the persecution in her country gave rise to a feeling of death knocking at her door. Besides, even if she did have to find her way back home, she could not pinpoint where England was located on the map. So many things, all at once, kept running through her head, and she must have fallen asleep out of exhaustion.

Sami woke her the next morning. He gave her a piece of paper with clear directions to the Home Office and the numbers of the buses she would need.

He told her she should always ask the bus driver for directions if she was unsure – 'they are usually very helpful'. He also put his home address and mobile number on the piece of paper. He reminded her that the same buses would get her back to his house if she had to return. He gave her a twenty pound note to add to the money that Jude had given her at the station. Esther gave her a good jacket as it was very cold; it was February. He took her to the bus stop where they had both alighted four days ago. She felt warm tears rolling down her cheeks. They had been so warm and kind to her, and she felt so unhappy. He took out his handkerchief and gently wiped away her tears, reassuring her that everything would be fine. He told her that she was welcome in his house at any time. She thanked him profusely, and they said their farewells. He looked sad when he said goodbye to her. The look in his eyes told her she might never see him again, or at least not for a very long time.

CHAPTER 2

A Secure Place

Deborah tried to think about the sad look on Sami's face and what it might mean. But she could not concentrate on that for long as she was anxious about what the future held for her at her unknown destination. When she got onto the bus, she showed the piece of paper to the driver with the description of the place she was heading to. He took the paper and looked at it carefully, and asked her to sit on one of the seats by the entrance. He told her he would let her know when she needed to get off. After a short ride the driver told her that the next stop was hers. He also reminded her that she needed to go across the road to catch the next bus, and pointed out the stop to her. She had been standing at the bus stop for less than five minutes when the next bus came. She got on, and again explained to the driver that she required assistance getting to her destination. He also showed her to a seat close to the front and said he would shout out when they got there. That made her feel easier, but her anxiety about the uncertainties did not go away: the Home Office and what she would find there, and the look on Sami's face. Then her thoughts rapidly switched to Jude. She wondered if he was thinking of her and where she was, or whether he had come back looking for her only to find that she had vanished without trace.

But she had followed Sami, and that was out of fear, so now she would never know. She was distracted by a loud noise at the entrance to the bus; it was the voice of an elderly lady. She was a very dark-skinned woman, even darker than Deborah, and she looked mysterious, too. This was about five stops after Deborah had got onto the bus, and she immediately started shouting at the driver: "Drive up, man!"

Every time the bus stopped to pick up passengers, she screeched, "Move the damn bus, move it, man!"

As the bus continued its route, she kept muttering to herself and pointing at the buildings as they passed. Her behavior was certainly unusual, Deborah thought. But the driver seemed completely unconcerned, and took no notice at all, so she assumed that he did not find this sort of performance at all unusual. After a few more stops, he told her in a kindly manner that this was where she should get off, and pointed at a large building on the other side of the road.

She stood gazing at the massive building across the road with amazement. It was a wonderful sight, but she did not stare for long as she immediately noticed a long queue of people at the far end of the building. These were mostly blacks, but there were also some coloured and white people. She thought to herself that they might be waiting for help, and so she approached the queue. A closer look convinced her that they might be in some kind of trouble. Most of them looked haggard and woebegone. There was a very strong stench which made her conclude that more than half of the people in the queue had not bathed for a long time.

Towards the end of the queue she saw a man and a woman talking to each other, and so she approached them. She stood behind them and after a minute or so she asked the woman if this was the right place to get help. The woman asked if she wanted to seek asylum, and Deborah explained that she had no home, and that someone had told her to come to this address. The woman confirmed that this was the place, but said that Deborah would have to stand at the rear of the line. She nodded, and went to the back of the line. The queue was getting longer as other people joined.

She asked herself why all these people needed help, and wondered where they came from.

The world must be in far more trouble than she thought. But she was certain about one thing: all these people did not have the same problems as hers. There were people all ages, and there were also families with kids. By the time she got into the building she had come to the conclusion that the Home Office should really be called the 'Rescue Centre' - if so many people were in the same state situation as her, then Heaven knows it could only be a rescue effort.

It was a good three hours before she finally got into the building. She thought to herself that it was a good thing that Sami had sent her off so early, because it seemed that not everybody would get to be seen that same day. The line did not seem to be getting any shorter. In fact, it was growing by the minute, and extended into the road. Another thought came to her: this might have been how or where Sami got help.

As she was still preoccupied with her thoughts, a voice told her to come forward. The man speaking to her was dressed like a police officer, with epaulettes on his shirt. She quickly moved forward. In response to his question, she told him her name. "How can we help?" he asked.

She told him that she really did need help: she had nowhere to go – she had neither had a place to sleep, nor food to eat, which was just what Sami had told her to say.

The man nodded, and asked if she wanted to seek asylum. She realized that this was the second time someone had used word asylum to her this morning. As she was still wondering what the word meant, the man asked another question.

"Do you have any form of identification?"

"What do you mean?" she said.

He told her he needed to see her passport, identity card, driver's license or birth certificate. She did not say a word, but indicated to him clearly that she had none of these documents. He told her that they had to be certain who she was, which meant they needed to see one of those documents before she would be allowed to speak to one of the immigration officers.

Deborah explained that she did not have any of the documents, and it would not have been possible to have them. She told him that she had come to this office because she had run away from her country, and if she had tried to bring her documents she would not have been able to get away. He looked at her for a second, and asked her to step aside so that the person behind her could come forward. She refused, and when he asked why, she asked what he would do if the building caught fire – would his first priority be to make sure he had all his documents or to run for his life? She then explained that where she came from, there was a fire - a fire that could burn all the life out of her, and papers to prove her identity were the last thing she would think of. He stared at her for a short while and then gave her a number, saying that she should listen for it to be called out. At this she breathed a sigh of relief.

The crowd inside the building was much bigger than the one outside. There were restaurants and shops, and she was beginning to feel hungry. She went into one of the shops and bought some biscuits and a can of coke, and sat herself in the waiting room.

After about two hours of waiting, her number was called. She got up and approached a black lady, who introduced herself as Justencia and explained that she was one of the immigration officers. She asked Deborah her name, where she came from and why she was in England. Deborah explained that she had belonged to a political movement in her home country, Cameroon, which the police regarded as a threat to the government and society. Members were hunted down and brutalized, and their lives were in danger. She described what she had suffered at the hands of the government, and how she had ended up with Jude. She also told her about the *Good Samaritan*, Sami, and how he had advised her to come to the Home Office. She showed Justencia Sami's address and phone number, and she wrote it down along with all the other details. Justencia then asked if she had left any luggage at Sami's house, which she had not, and said she was asking because Deborah would not be going back there. It was clear that she had no doubt that Sami was a good man. But although he had been so nice and friendly, it was a criminal offence for someone to house a person without official immigrant status. Deborah did not understand what Justencia meant by immigrant status, but nodded to indicate that she was listening.

Justencia told her that arrangements would be made for her to stay at a nearby guest house for the night. She was to report to the same office before 6 a.m., where she would be given further information and directions. Justencia then stood up and asked her to wait for a minute and not to go away. She disappeared behind a counter, and came back a moment later with some papers. These contained directions to the guest house and instructions to report to the Home Office again very early in the morning, as she had already said. Deborah was worried sick that she might not be able to find the guest house, and would therefore have to spend the night on the street. The map Justencia had given her showed buildings and the names of streets, and she had circled the guest house. But Deborah could not work out where the Home Office was on the map, and that was her starting point, so the map was useless to her. Justencia also warned her that returning to Sami's house would land him in big trouble with the state because she did not have official immigrant status, as she had already said.

Deborah stepped outside into the cold air wondering which direction to go, for the paper she had been given still made no sense. She turned left as she came out of the building, and then decided to look back. But she saw that everyone who left the building was heading in the opposite direction, and so she retraced her steps and followed them. The guest house was actually just ten minutes' walk from the Home Office, but that was not at all clear because the map was full of drawings of buildings and trees and all sorts of landmarks. So when she did eventually find it, she could not imagine why Justencia had felt she needed a pile of papers for a simple ten-minute walk. But Deborah was quite sure of one thing: the name Justencia sounded stupid. How could such a pretty woman have a name like that and keep a straight face? 'Justencia' Indeed!

CHAPTER 3

The Guest House

She rang the bell at the guest house twice, and after a while she heard footsteps approaching. She prepared to explain what she was there for. When the door opened she realized she would not have to say a word, as a strange voice called from upstairs in a strange language to the man at the door. After they had talked for a few seconds the man said 'Azylum Sicker'. He opened the door wide, and in a strange English accent invited her in, forcing a smile from the side of his mouth that made his face look very unfriendly. She stepped inside and he immediately shut the door. He might have been of Asian origin because he looked like one of the actors in the numerous Indian movies she had watched long ago as a kid. Only this guy was a bit older than the actors she remembered, and he had quite a beard on his chin. While he was closing the door she heard his strange English accent again, but this time his question was directed at her and it startled her: "Wat contry are u furum?"

When she told him, he said, "Oh, Kameroon". And then, "Kameroon play good football", and asked, "Plenty people here from Kameroon?"

Deborah was not sure exactly what he wanted, and so she did not respond. But he carried on anyway: "Afrika many, many problems, eh?" Deborah gave a small sigh and wondered to herself what he could mean by 'Afrika many problems'. She had seen people from all over the world at the 'Rescue Centre', and it seemed as though there were more people from his part of the world than Africans – so what could he have been talking about? "Come, I show you the room", and he led her to a door, where he turned to

17

face her and said, "When you arrive the contry?" That almost knocked her off balance, and she looked at him again for a few seconds, but all she could see was the beard. It made him look like one of the horned, sheep-like animals she knew from her country. When she asked if it was her room, he just nodded. She thanked him, stepped inside and closed the door behind her.

She could not help but notice how small the room was - everything about it was so tiny. The table and chair were so small that she could only think they had been made for a child. A single bed forced into a little corner of the room was also so small that for a moment she wondered if she would fit in. But what really struck her was the cold in the room. It was February, and it was so cold that she did not want to sit down. Reeling from the intensity of the cold, she dashed out of the room shouting, "Is there anybody here?" After letting out two screams she saw the man marching towards her. He asked her to hush as some of the guests were already asleep, and she stood still, not saying anything. He gave her a rather strange look, demanding to know what the matter was and asking if she did not like the room. She thought beggars can't be choosers, but as he was obviously expecting a response, she told him that the room was perfect and she was grateful for it, but it was the cold. She felt she simply could not survive in such a temperature.

He went past her into the room, and as she heard him cursing under his breath that the room was not supposed to be that cold. He then paused for a while in the tiny space in the center of the room looking confused, before walking towards the window. He let out a big sigh of relief and explained apologetically that the cleaners had forgotten to close the window after cleaning the room a couple of days back. She told him that she had needed to call someone's attention to the cold in the room so that she would not turn into a pillar of ice before dawn. He told her there was another room she could use, as it would take quite a while to warm hers up. So she followed him to the next room. As they made their way to the new room she asked if he help her to wake her up in the morning as she needed to be at the Home Office by 6 a.m. He told her he would not be able to come and wake her up himself, but he had something he could give her that would help her. She was already shaking her head in disapproval as if to say she did not want to anything to drink or eat to help wake her up when he hurriedly said he had an alarm clock. He offered it to her and told her to leave it on top of the table in her room.

The alarm clock was like a tiny jewellery box, but she was shocked at the amount of noise such a little thing could produce. The alarm was set for 5 a.m. to give her enough time to get ready. When it went off in the morning she almost jumped out of her bed because the sound was so loud. But there was a problem: the man had forgotten to show her how to turn off the alarm. She had no idea where he was sleeping, and so she could not find him. But then, she really did not want to wake him up just to turn an alarm off. She had looked all over the tiny box, but could not find a button to turn it off, and it was really loud. All she could think of was to cover it with her pillow to smother the noise. She left at 5.40, wondering what he would think of her when he found the alarm still ringing under her pillow.

Deborah had been locked up too many times in her life, and she would not willingly have allowed herself to enter any environment which did not allow her to come and go freely. If she had thought for a second that on her arrival at the 'rescue centre' that morning she would be grabbed,

19

detained and caged up, she swore by the grave of her grandfather that she would not have returned.

A lot of things happened and everything moved really fast when she got to the Home Office that morning. Within an hour she had confirmed her name, had been photographed and finger-printed, and had been securely locked up in a tiny room. The people who put her in the little room said they were the police, and told her they had done this for her own protection. She almost believed them because they were different, very different in the manner they spoke to her, and this showed respect. What is more, they tried to explain in detail everything they were doing, and also tried to crack jokes to make her feel relaxed. They were neatly dressed, and she loved the way they carried their guns on their hips - she even thought it was a bit sexy.

But any form of locking up is bad for the human mind. The mere presence of the police gave Deborah a bad feeling, and she started weeping. The officer in charge opened the door and stepped into the little room; he tried to persuade her not to cry, and she asked again why they had to lock her in the room. He explained that soon she would be taken to another place where she would be questioned in detail. This would help them decide whether she needed help or not. But at the moment they, the police officers, were just following procedures. She looked at the officer and told herself this man would never understand her: he looked healthy and comfortable, and she felt for sure that he had never cried, gone to bed hungry or had a whole day without food, or indeed had had any form of pain inflicted on him in his entire life: so how could he possibly understand? And so if she said she really understood the tiniest bit of the explanation he had just given her, she would be lying. Yes, she had heard what he said and could even have repeated it a million times - but what he had just told her about process and procedures was something she honestly would never understand.

CHAPTER 4

Cambridge

The ride to the town called Cambridge was very quiet, so much so that she slept most of the way. At Cambridge she would be questioned, drilled and examined until whoever was in charge was fully satisfied, so she had been told. The two officers in charge of her ride tried to be friendly, but she kept quiet. They wanted to know where she came from and what she was doing in the country, but she was not interested. They had her all caged up and separated from them in the vehicle, with a tiny hole between them. It was as if she was on the FBI's 'most wanted' list, yet they were acting as if they did not have a care in the world. She had no way of knowing whether whatever she said or did would be used against her in a court of law or whatever detention station they were taking her to. To her, right now, they were the enemy. So she made a promise to herself that until she knew and understood what they wanted from her, she was going to keep quiet. She had been in situations like this, far too many times. She knew silence was golden, as there is so much more one can do with keeping your mouth shut.

How could she have known that simply asking for help would turn into such a drama? Had she said something to the Justencia woman – the 'Immigration Officer' – that made them lock her up, and now subject her to this interminable ride to nowhere? She would have to wait and see.

They must have arrived in Cambridge at nightfall, as everything was very dark. She was escorted into a large room that looked like the reception area of an office. A female officer approached them with a warm smile, as if to say 'well done' for catching a dangerous criminal, and they handed her a pile of papers that Deborah thought must contain all her details. There was also a large group of people in the room who looked just as bewildered and confused as herself. The officers who had escorted her had a brief chat with the female officer, then asked Deborah to make herself comfortable. She was also shown a refrigerator and told to eat whatever she wanted from it if she was hungry. Before they said their goodbyes, they told her that someone would come for her and that she should just be patient.

After an hour or so, the female officer who had collected her details came and called her name. She stood up and walked towards her, and was ushered into a room. She was told that she was at the Oakington Reception Centre. The lady read something out from a piece of paper and told her they were her rights. She nodded to indicate that she had understood. Then the officer searched her quickly and made a detailed list of all her possessions. She handed her over to another officer, who escorted her to a sleeping area.

When she woke in the morning and saw she was surrounded by other people in the sleeping area - it was like being at college again. The only difference was that the people she was sharing this dormitory with were not friends or even people from her own county. They were from all nations and continents, including some whose origins she really could not fathom. It was obvious that they had different reasons for being locked up at the centre, and she discovered that not everyone had just arrived from their own country. Most people were already living and working in England, but unfortunately did not have the right residence permits. There was a woman and a man who had been brought in in their wedding outfits a day after they had arrived. Apparently the marriage had not been for love, and there had been a tip-off by an informant. So they were arrested in the middle of the ceremony. The man was African, and had no immigration status. He had paid the woman, who was from France, a ridiculous amount of money to pretend she was his bride so that he could be regularized.

The first person Deborah got to know at Oakington was a Chinese woman. She made her smile and laugh at will. Her attempt at speaking English was hilarious, but she was determined. She was a sweet soul, and she made several attempts to teach Deborah Chinese. But it was so difficult to pronounce the words, and whenever Deborah tried to say something it made her sound like a professional mourner, and so she gave up.

A few days later she became friends with another woman, this time from the Middle East. They met in the dining room, where the woman was battling with indecision about where to sit for lunch with her two little girls. She informed Deborah that the day before she had been brought from another centre to this one, but her quarters were different from Deborah's as families had privileges. When they chatted she could understand this woman much better than her Chinese friend. However, this woman told her that she expected to be accompanied by someone to translate her every word whenever she was called up for an interview by the officials. Yet she said she wished that was not the case, because on occasion she could clearly hear the translator telling the official a totally different from what she had actually said. Deborah told her that she had the right to object, but she replied that she could not do this as she herself had asked for a translator because she was worried that her English was not too good.

Deborah felt genuine pity for her as she looked worried. She had told Deborah that she could not afford to be returned to her home land, for that would mean that her two girls would have to suffer the gruesome pains of circumcision. Deborah looked at her, genuinely shocked at what she had said. She said that she herself had undergone this operation, although against her wish. So she had made a personal promise to herself: she would never let anyone in her care be subjected to such dehumanizing treatment. Deborah was still in shock, as in own country circumcision was only for men. She could not imagine what could be plucked from a woman's genitals, as there did not seem to be anything there. Inquisitive, she pressed on to find out what exactly was being chopped off and why. The woman told her that female genital mutilation was a massive issue in her world. Apparently it was difficult to estimate the number of women across the world who may have suffered as a result of this terrible act. The World Health Organization has estimated numbers the figure as high as 120 million women in more than 30 countries. There are no medical, hygiene or health reasons for women to be subjected to the gruesome ordeal, but it persists as a deep-rooted traditional practice in many African and Middle Eastern countries. Deborah gazed at her in disbelief, not quite sure of what to make of what she was saying, but nodding so she would continue.

The woman from the Middle East explained that this age-old tradition is commonly performed by traditional birth attendants, who are local women or men, or by female family members. The circumcisers do not have any medical training or anatomical knowledge of the vulva, and they usually perform the act without anaesthesia and without sterilizing the equipment used. It is not uncommon for those who perform mutilations to cut or damage more of the genital area than they intend. The practice of female circumcision has for a long time been a source of controversy, pain and disagreement within the communities where it is practiced. Men have used it to enhance their supremacy over women. She said there was hope that the practice would come to an end sooner rather than later, as in recent years there has been a real push towards the abolition of all practices that are deemed shameful to women. And foremost amongst these practices is female genital mutilation - a practice which involves cutting away part of a woman's entire clitoris.

This has not however been accepted by the men, who usually are in the dominant position within the village assembly. To them, and most especially the community's rulers, it is a key aspect of their stranglehold over women. Women are all considered children of the ruler's household, just because they are born in the village. The woman said that in recent years associations that have spoken up and are still speaking against such practices have been faced with a lot of hostility from the rulers. They have also had opposition from men, who are usually a gang of thugs who take full advantage of the ruler's favors and are prepared to do whatever he demands of them. She confessed that during and after her ordeal she had almost died because she was bleeding so heavily and had had numerous infections. To make matters worse, immediately after circumcision the victim has to move back to her husband's house, and he may still use her for his pleasure night after night, making it very hard for the wounds to heal.

Deborah clenched her teeth together and felt goose bumps all over her body. She could see in her mind's eye the agony this woman must have been through, and one could still see the furrows of pain across her forehead. The woman said she was twenty-three years old, but the untold suffering she had been through made her look as if she was in her mid-forties. Fortunately for her, she had given birth to two lovely little girls. She had vowed that she was not going to let some haughty, heartless men take it upon themselves to rip these little girls' insides apart. Deborah asked her if she had been as young as her daughters were now when she was circumcised, and she said she had actually been a year younger than her second girl - just eight years old. Deborah had always thought that her own childhood had been traumatic, but she now realized that it paled in comparison to the suffering her new friend had undergone as a child. She thanked the woman for sharing her story, and it was clear to her that she was exceptionally courageous and brave.

Apparently, ten per cent of girls and women die from the short-term complications of female genital mutilation. The common complications are hemorrhage, shock and infection. Such a percentage of deaths she thought was very high, so why can world leaders not do anything about it? This is ten per cent of girls, woman and mothers dying in vain and for no just course. That was sad - very sad indeed! To Deborah's shock, when she dug deeper into the subject she learned that it was a practice in her own country, too. How come she had never heard of it? She was told that in a village called Mfuni it was a popular practice. That was where there had been a clash in the past when the bishop of the Littoral and South West division of the Eglise du Christianisme Celeste was refused an audience by the chief when he came to inaugurate the Women's Centre which had been donated to the village by the church, and it was because the pastor of the village church was against all those involved with and usually preached against female genital mutilation. Knowing for sure that this was a practice in her own country was disturbing. Deborah was shocked, and she honestly did not want to know any more. Well, maybe not now.

A bell was sounded for every single activity at the Oakington Centre. Breakfast, lunch and supper were not an obligation, but there was plenty to eat. However, food was not a priority, particularly as Deborah had more urgent needs and more important matters to see to. She hated the Centre announcement system. They always used it when someone's attention was required or if they had something important to say. It was ear-splitting. Announcements were made four or five times before people clearly understood what they were about, and that was because of the noise generated. The irony was that the system made a mockery of its original purpose, as rather than getting peoples' attention it could deafen them. Deborah swore she was definitely going to be deaf by the time she left the Oakington Centre - the bell was just so loud. If anything could wake up the dead, then it was this bell. She believed that the bell was made so loud on purpose, for she had never heard anything like it in her life.

After her first night she was given a list of the activities which took place at the Centre. One could go to the gym, there was a library which she was interested in, and also evening church service. She attended the church services as she felt she needed it. In desolate times such as these, only prayers and constant meditation could offer consolation. There was also a coffee, tea and chocolate hour, and truly this made her wonder what all the food was for. She thought maybe the people running the centre knew that where their residents came from there were no such privileges, or perhaps they thought that people might want to seek respite from their desperate situation in food. Or it could even be the case that the availability of food

28

was based on the belief that 'a hungry man is an angry man'.

Deborah's special code, room number and bed number were called over the Centre announcement system. She dashed to the reception and was told her solicitor had called that he would be at the main waiting room in five minutes. A solicitor's visit was a top priority, so she was told. She hurried up to her room, picked up her coat and ran to the waiting room. The room was empty and very quiet, so she sat herself down on one of the chairs.

CHAPTER 5

The Solicitor

"My name is John, John Biggs. I believe you are Deborah?" She nodded and murmured, "Yes, Deborah". John told her straight away that he would be representing her and helping her with her asylum application. He also informed her that she would have to tell him in detail why she had made the decision to come in to Britain. Without a detailed reason he was sorry, but he would not be able to help her. She looked him straight in the face from the edge of the chair in the small waiting room. He was very tall, and it occurred to her that his name should have been Long John and not John Biggs, as he was truly long. He looked very calm and had fine blue eyes that were almost intimidating. She asked herself if these people were ever going to help her. It had been four days since she had gone to the Home Office in Croydon to seek help - and all they had done was to move her from one place to another. Also, John would be the fourth person to whom she would be telling the story of her life. Each and every one of them had threatened that if she didn't tell them the details of her flight to England then they could not help her.

While preoccupied with these thoughts, her expression must have told John that she did not trust him. He must have noticed this, because he quickly moved towards her and whispered, "I am your lawyer, and you should not be afraid to talk to me." He also reassured her that he had listened to and helped lots of people in the same kind of situation. She gently asked if they were going to hand her back to the Cameroon police. For if they did, she would be slaughtered, and she did not want to die now. He reassured her that no one would do that - if anyone wanted to kill her they would protect her. When John talked about 'protecting' her, it sounded so real. It reminded her that nobody had used that word to her, nor had anyone actually taken steps to protect her unless they would get something out of it themselves.

She thought again about why she was in England and her current predicament. Vivid thoughts of all the troubles she had met in her life filled her memory - they were so vivid, and she could replay everything like a movie. Everything came back in a flash! The rape itself, the ill-treatment from her parents when they found that she was pregnant – the memories were overpowering. She could still see in her mind's eye the legs of the tall soldier approaching the cave, his huge body pressing her into the bare African soil, his disgusting odour - she could even smell that again. Her mother, oh her dear mother: the look of disappointment and disdain on her face that seemed to say she no longer wanted this daughter. Then the beatings, when her mother held her firm so she could not escape while her father used whatever item he could lay his hands on to bring down on her with all his strength. She remembered how defenceless and frail she had been, not truly understanding the reasons for all the torture. Then the fear that if she chose to tell them what had happened and explain it, nobody would accept and believe her story. And even if they did choose to believe her, she might still be banished by her family for the shame of having been raped. 'Why *our* daughter?' they would wonder. Had there been no other young girls around that this crazed soldier could have preyed on? Had she been born to meet such a fate? The un-answered questions would go on until they had no choice but to expel her from their midst.

She also remembered the torment and ill-treatment she had received at the hands of her government in her effort to right the wrong that one of their soldiers had done her. She thought of Jude and his promise to arrange her safe passage to London - his assurance that he would provide accommodation, a job and a better life. Yet he had deserted her in the middle of nowhere a day after they had arrived in England. She felt sweat on her brow and tears running down her cheeks. She shivered at her thoughts, and John Biggs asked her if she was alright. She looked at him and said, "Do you really want to know why I ran away from my country?" He nodded to show that he did, and she indicated where she would like him to sit. She then said to him, "I will tell - and you are the first soul I am telling this to".

Even though she had decided to tell her story, she was a bit hesitant. She had kept this secret to herself over the years, and she saw him just as another man. Just another man, she thought: all the problems she had suffered had been caused by men – so what difference would it make? But as these thoughts ran through her mind, he asked her a question that changed everything. Did she have any family back home, he asked, and did she have kids? She responded that her parents and sisters were alive, and that she had a child who did not know his father. He said gently, "Please tell me about it."

She told him that being raped was terrible, but knowing that you have been raped by an enemy was even worse. As she lay there and the black giant had penetrated her body, what kept her alive was the strong conviction that if she survived the ordeal she would never see him again. When John asked why she was so convinced, she said it was because he was not from the same region of the country as her. She was very sure about that, because people like her from southern Cameroon did not speak much French, and even if they did, it was not with a refined accent. Yet as he had held her down, he had mumbled incantations like

32

those used by witch doctors, but in French. His entire body was as dark as the charcoal under her mother's cooking pot, his eyes were very red, and he was exceptionally tall. As she was very young, just turning 11, she did not really understand what this man mountain was doing to her. But she vividly remembered how badly it had hurt - so badly that her strength was exhausted and she fainted.

Before she went on with her story, she gave John a brief history of her country – that would help him to form a better understanding of what she was going to tell him. She also encouraged him to ask for a fuller explanation if he felt he needed it.

Deborah grew up in Mamfe, a small city in the south of Cameroon. It is actually the oldest city in that part of the country. There is linguistic evidence to indicate that the areas now known as Cameroon and Eastern Nigeria were previously under Bantu rule. After the 12th century AD, the organized Islamic states of the Sudanic belt, especially those of the Kanem and Fulani peoples, at times ruled the grasslands of northern Cameroon. Small chiefdoms dominated the western highlands. Portuguese travelers and other Europeans established contact with Cameroon mainly for coastal trade and the acquisition of slaves between the 16th and the early 19th centuries. Although no permanent settlements were maintained then, they played havoc with ethnic groupings and with the district, regional, cultural, religious and political traditions of the country.

The modern history of Cameroon began in 1884, when the territory came under German rule after the explorer Gustav Nachtigal negotiated protectorate treaties with local chiefs. Although British missionaries had been active in the area since 1845, the UK recognized the German protectorate, which was called Kamerun. This included areas that were later to become British Cameroon and French Cameroun. Cameroon might not have been occupied if it had not been for the greed of the Adolf Hitler, for as a German colony the country became a battleground. After the joint effort that saw the Germans defeated in Cameroon by Britain and France in 1919, the country was sliced like a piece of bread into two unequal sections. The part of the country which was contiguous with eastern Nigeria, comprising a fifth of the former German Kamerun, was assigned to the United Kingdom, and the remaining four fifths was assigned to France under the League of Nations mandates.

France made notable contributions to the development of their part of the territory. Agriculture was expanded, industries were introduced, roads were built, medical services were expanded, and more schools were established. Political freedom was restricted, and the system of compulsory labor introduced by the Germans continued. In August 1940, Colonel Philippe Leclerc, an envoy of General Charles de Gaulle, landed at Douala and seized the territory for the Free French. The birth of the Fourth French Republic and the UN trusteeship in 1946 signified a new era for the territory. French Cameroun was granted representation in the French National Assembly and the Council of the Republic. An elected territorial assembly was instituted and political parties were recognized, thus establishing a basis for Cameroonian nationalism.

On 1 January 1960, Cameroun became an independent republic. The political system in Cameroon is classed as a 'dictatorial democracy', or what we call 'new dictatorship'

To Deborah, Cameroon was privately owned. Despite the fact that democratic reform began in 1990 with the legalization of political parties, the Cameroon National

Democratic Party (CPDM) seemed to be the sole political party. Political power remained firmly in the hands of President Paul Biya and a small circle of members of his political party and his own ethnic group.

One result of the division of the country between Britain and France was that established regional boundaries and the differences between them were simply ignored. Imagine a once united Cameroon forced to become two separate nations, each with its own borders and border passes. The inhabitants of the two countries had to learn strange and different languages, and their mother tongues were banished. So when the opportunity came for reunification in 1961, it was something of a shock for southern Cameroonians to realise they were now being reunited with strangers. At this point John Biggs interrupted, asking what Deborah meant by 'reunite with strangers'. She told him that those in the French-governed part of the country had learnt a new culture and system of government, just as the British Cameroonians had. One thing the British Cameroonians had not realised was that they were now in a minority, as four fifths of the country was French. From the outset of the reunification process they realised they had become strangers to one another. As if this was not enough, there was also back-stabbing, and the legacy of the French 'laissez-faire' attitude and other widespread problems emerged. Ever since the reunification of the British and French territories of Cameroon, the minority southern Cameroonians have known no peace. Way before Deborah was born in 1980, pressure had been mounting between the two territories even though they had officially been reunified via a referendum.

On the day of the rape incident, the mounting anger among southern Cameroonians, and especially among university graduates and the unemployed, had erupted like a volcano. There was a riot which was planned and well organised, and violence was spreading across the country like magma flowing down a mountain slope. Deborah still had vivid memories. Yet it was a very quiet and peaceful day at our lady seat of all Saints, the small college she was attending in the small town of Fontem. Neither the pupils nor the teachers were aware that the riot was becoming chaotic and violent. Fontem is no more than 200 miles from Mamfe, her home town. Seat of All Saints College had been recommended to her father because of its outstanding results. The school was owned and governed by a Christian organization called 'All Saints'. The school had links with the Roman Catholic Church and the mother branch was in Rome. Its reputation was very high, with results second to none in the country and exceptional standards of behaviour. Admission to All Saints College was on merit, and it was not possible to gain entrance through connections or corruption. So she was a very proud little girl when she passed her entrance exams and was admitted. John said that she must have been very excited, too. She told him that she was even more proud of herself when her parents had dropped her off on her first day September 23rd 1990.

Little did she know that her pride and excitement would soon turn into the greatest nightmare of her life! The riot of the disgruntled southern Cameroonians had been planned to coincide with the National Day celebration held on the 20th of May each year to mark the independence of Cameroon. The entire school had gathered in the main dining hall at breakfast time. Just after prayers and before the meal started there was a big bang. She heard someone screaming, "Soldiers - run for your dear life". She could not remember how she got out of the hall as there was a stampede; with everyone struggling to get out at once. She remembered thinking to herself that the only place she could run to was a small forest at the back of the main school building, and that was the only thing she could think of. One had to cross a tiny stream to get there. It had a small cave that she and her friends particularly liked to play in. She reached the cave quickly and ran inside, but unbeknown to her she had been seen by one of the soldiers. She was terrified when she heard the heavy footsteps approaching, and held her breath and stood still. She could hear herself gasping for air as the soldier's legs appeared visible just outside the cave. He stood there for a while. She put her head between her knees, covering it with her arms, and prayed to God for protection.

Her prayer certainly did not get to God on time. All she remembered when she awoke was the pain from the bruises that covered the inside of her legs. She remembered the beginning of the ordeal clearly, but she must have fainted half way through, for she no longer knew how it had ended. John grumbled something under his breath and when Deborah looked up at him, she noticed his face had gone red. She quickly asked if he was ok. He did not respond, but held his fist as tight as if he was about to punch someone. When he did open his mouth, what came out was 'bloody animal!' Then he asked Deborah to carry on.

Deborah's tiny body felt agonisingly heavy when she tried to stand up in the cave. She managed to get on her knees and crawl to the mouth of the cave, and with both hands she held fast on to the cave wall and stood up. The immediate pain in her underbelly was excruciating, and she was still bleeding. The midday birds were already singing and flitting from one tree to another. The squirrels were gathering dead leaves and plants, too. Deborah watched for a while - a sight she was so familiar with. One of the squirrels danced towards her as if expecting to be fed, as Deborah and her friends regularly came to this spot with peanuts and bread crumbs. When it realised that she was not going to give it any food, it look at her sternly and dashed off into the bushes. Deborah sensed that even the little animal must have realised something was terribly wrong - it had never before run off when there was any hope of being fed, especially after such a dance performance. She looked up at the sun, which had barely managed to pierce through the clouds although it was past midday. Was this a reflection of the ordeal she had undergone?

Deborah knew she needed to help herself, so she took a step towards the little stream despite the pain, staggering but determined to get to the girls' boarding house. As she approached the hostel, the silence was oppressive. The buildings of the school were like a ghost town. There were suitcases left half open outside, and bags and books were littered everywhere. It was if a gang of robbers had attacked them in the night. Had the soldiers been bent on plunder, too? She stepped on a shoe lying on the ground, and when she picked it up realised that it belonged to a friend. She stared at it, hoping her classmate was alright. She eventually managed to get to her room, and it was only when she took off her clothes and torn underwear that she realised the gravity of what had happened to her. Her body was covered with cuts and scratches, and she was shaking with fear and in a state of complete shock. She wept quietly, sitting on her bed and trying to work out what had happened to her. What she knew immediately was that nobody must see her in this state. Although she was scared out of her wits, she decided to stay in the school for two more days before heading home to her parents.

CHAPTER 6

Grandpa

Deborah's parents were very grateful to see her at home two days after all the rioting as they were aware of the political upheavals. They had experienced more of the rioting and fighting, as there had been more happening and even gunfire in the larger city. At home Deborah was unable to walk or eat. She was severely bruised and was hurting very badly. She hoped and prayed she would wake up and find that it had all just been a nightmare. In her bed, she would curl up in a ball, fearfully re-living the actions of the tall dark soldier all night long .Then she would wake up screaming and sweltering as though she was being pursued by an evil spirit. Finally, she came to the conclusion that what the soldier had done to her must have been something very terrible. The pains in and around her private area were almost unbearable. Her strange feelings and her fear made her feel sure she could tell nobody. She knew that describing what had happened to her or talking about the pains she felt could get her into big trouble.

She cried most nights for weeks on end. She knew how awful it was to be a rape victim. She knew there had been cases where girls had been disowned by their parents for saying that they had been raped. Who in her community would believe her story? Some might be tempted to listen sympathetically - but who had the guts to stand up to the men in their society? In addition, rape was seen as a bad omen, even to the extent that nobody wants to be associated with the victim - not even the parents. Both the victim and the whole subject of rape is taboo.

Knowing definitely that describing what had happened or even mentioning it was out of the question, she resorted to hot water and salt to heal her bruises. Deborah's mother was very concerned that she could not walk properly and as she could not tell the truth, she lied that she had been knocked down when she was running away from the soldiers, and her legs and hips had been badly hurt. Within a month she was better, however, and able to go out again. But as the days went by she became sick, vomiting and not eating properly and that aroused her mother's attention again. Although she still did not say anything and was trying to go about her daily duties as normal, her mother somehow knew all was not well with her, and decided to probe more closely.

She started observing Deborah closely, trying to decide for herself what could be wrong with her. Two to three months after her return from school, she called Deborah into her room just after their evening meal. When they were safely in the room, she looked at her daughter, raising her head and speaking in a voice which was almost like a whisper. "Debbie", she asked, "who got you pregnant?" Deborah gave her a confused look, so she repeated the question, this time more clearly and with greater urgency. "I said who got you pregnant?" Confused, Deborah repeated the word 'pregnant'. This time her mother looked her straight in the eye and said, "Yes – pregnant!" Afraid to give a direct answer, Deborah shivered violently as if to deny that she was pregnant and to indicate that she did not know what her mother was talking about. Her mother decided that she had no alternative but to take her to the hospital for some tests first thing in the morning.

Deborah was genuinely confused about her mother's questions, for it had still not occurred to her that she could be pregnant. She knew about pregnancy in very general terms, because she had seen her mother pregnant with her

40

siblings, and women from the neighborhood with swollen stomachs, which she had been told meant that they were pregnant with babies. But she was not really sure of exactly how and why one got pregnant. So she continued to insist that she was not pregnant and that she had not done anything she should not have done. Her mother's response was, "Let's see what the doctors say!"

Arrangements were made immediately for Deborah to go and live with her mother's relatives in the village until her baby was born, as her parents did not want the news of her pregnancy to spread and ruin any future prospects of her finding a husband. They also not want to be seen as bad parents.

Her grandmother had suffered from diabetes and had died three years earlier but her grandfather was still alive and was very happy to see Deborah. He was not happy with the bruises and cuts he saw on her face and arms, and he immediately demanded that she should tell him where she got them from, so she said that it was her parents who had done it. He stared into the distance for a while as if in a trance, and then swallowed hard. But he did not say anything more about the subject. Once the welcome rituals were complete, she handed him the letter her parents had told her to give him which described her situation and contained a promise that they would visit regularly. Grandpa was very quiet for a while after reading the letter. He had always been a man of few words, and restricted himself to saying only what was necessary. He was a very honorable man, and his honesty had earned him a place as the leader of the councillors in the village.

He went into his hut, and after a short he called for Deborah. He showed her into her room and told her that he was going to arrange it so she would be comfortable. He watched her closely again, and smiled as he said, "Everything will be OK, child". This was completely in contrast to the way she had been treated by her parents. The beatings, verbal abuse and everything else she had gone through overwhelmed her, and she started weeping. Grandpa immediately pulled her into his arms and squeezed her. "I do not want to know how you got yourself into this situation, my child" he said, "but I can assure you that you will be OK". He held her for a while longer, and then told her to go and unpack her suitcase and then get freshened up so she could have something to eat.

Within a week Deborah had settled in properly. Everything was done differently in the village, from travelling to preparing a meal. Walking was the only way you could get from one place to another. No one owned a vehicle in the community - not even a bicycle -, but that could be down to the fact that her grandfather's village was in a mountainous area. It was so hilly that Deborah was scared that someday the hills might fall down on them while they were asleep. Even though her grandmother had died some years ago, she   discovered that Grandpa kept collecting new wives and now he had five woman married to him. Two of these wives were much younger than Deborah's mother .With these young ladies in the compound it was easy for Grandpa to arrange things so that Deborah did not have to perform any difficult tasks like carrying loads on her head or going to fetch water in the valleys.

Deborah's parents regularly sent money for her upkeep. The money was very welcome as it enabled her to follow in her grandmother's footsteps and occasionally go to the local markets to get basic necessities for herself. Grandpa's youngest wife Sarah gave her advice on how to make the pregnancy as easy as possible. As the time approached, Sarah told her to climb the hills twice a week

42

to expand her pelvis and thus make the actual birth easier. Sarah told Deborah that if she had a husband, he would also help expand her pelvis through regular sexual activity. But for a single pregnant woman the only way to ease the birth was by walking up and down the hills. Her step grandmothers cared for as if she were their own, reassuring her that everything would work out well and watching over her like a princess. Deborah felt so welcome and at home that when her parents failed to visit her as they had promised, it simply did not matter to her, and she did not wonder why they stayed away; Grandpa also did not seem concerned, as they were all getting on fine.

How Deborah loved and missed those times she spent in her mother's village. The evenings were the best and most exciting times, when everybody gathered round a big fire and told all sorts of stories. The scariest stories were about people dying and being buried, and then coming back as ghosts for one reason or another. She remembered one evening, when after the story-telling session she could not walk back to her Grandpa's hut because she had been so frightened. In one story about a man who had died a while back in the village; his family kinsmen did not believe he had died of natural courses, as it had all happened very suddenly. So they buried him with a cutlass and knives, and after a day he was out hunting for his killer and almost everyone in the village saw him.

Sometimes, after the delicious midday meal, Grandpa also told tales of slavery and the slave trade. He recounted how one afternoon his own grandfather (Deborah's great-great-grandfather) was returning home from his aunt's house in a nearby village when he was snatched away by slave traders. Grandpa's parents and other family members did not know what had happened to him, so they believed he had had an accident, or maybe that he had been eaten by a wild animal. His family and the other villagers went into mourning for him, and dug a grave in which they buried some of his clothes as a sign of remembrance. But after 21years he reappeared and told them the story of the slave hunters, and how he had been taken all the way to Egypt. He had been convinced he would never see his family again, but after many years slavery and the slave trade were abolished. Confused and penniless, he lived and worked with a very nice Muslim family and was converted to Islam. After saving enough money he told them he had to return home to his family so that they would know he was still alive. Grandpa told her that for a long while after his grandfather returned home and even after he himself was born, his grandfather continued to practice the Muslim faith. That included not eating pork, as in Islamism forbid the eating of pig meat.

Deborah gave birth on the 17th of January, 1992. It was a little boy. Her own body was not fully formed, and could not handle the intensity of the pre-birth pains. It was a very difficult birth, and Deborah passed out and went into a coma. During the two weeks she was in the coma her step grandmothers took turns to nurse her damaged pelvis. Her little boy was breast-fed by two other relatives who had also just given birth. She came round after two weeks and a couple of days, and was surprised to see so many people around her. Sarah, Grandpa's youngest wife, explained to her how she had struggled with the pain and had blacked out just as the baby was coming out. She also made explained to her that it was the tradition that her baby could be fed by any nursing mothers in the family. Even when she came round she still could not produce any breast milk, and both Grandpa's daughters took turns to breast-feed her son. Deborah was very grateful to them, as she knew breast milk was her son's only chance of survival, for without it he would have had no resistance to bacteria.

Grandpa told Deborah that he had not informed her parents of the birth of her child. He had to wait before sending word because of the difficulties surrounding the birth of her child. As well as that, tradition demanded that if she had not come round within a month then the elders would have assisted her to come to permanent rest. He could not send a message to her parents as soon as she gave birth because he was unsure of what would happen to her. Deborah, feeling sorry for herself, demanded to know if anyone had ever been in her situation before, and what the villagers or elders had done. Grandpa confessed to her that there had been many similar cases - and many had not been as lucky as she was. In his time there had been countless young women who had been buried after a month because they had fainted during childbirth. Seeing the shock on Deborah's face, he insisted that this was the tradition, and nothing could be done about it. He explained that some women develop too fast, and that is mistaken for maturity, so they are sent off to get married. Then, when they eventually get pregnant and their tender bodies cannot stand the pain of childbirth, the spirits from the world of the dead slowly steal their breath. Then he held her hands and squeezed them, telling her he knew she was stronger than the spirits, and he had never doubted that she was going to come around. Deborah did not know what to make of all this, but to tell the truth she was shaken to the core. How could someone be buried alive? They say it is 'the tradition' – but what about the cruelty of it all?

At this point John decided that he could not take any more of what she was telling him, and he asked to step outside for a couple of minutes. After a few seconds she heard him on his phone in the corridor, but could not decipher what he was saying; then he was silent for a while before returning to the little interview room. He told her he had made arrangements to come back by 9 a.m. the next day to see her. Now it was Deborah who felt exhausted and worn out, and all she did was to nod. "See you tomorrow!" he said, but as he picked up his briefcase and took moved towards the door, she said, "I also killed a man!" He hesitated momentarily, without turning round, and hurried through the door and disappeared.

When she stepped out of the interview room to go to her custody quarters, she realized that it had gone pitch black outside. Although it was winter and she had been told that nightfall was earlier, she wondered how long she had been in that small room talking to a total stranger. She went straight to bed and for the first time in a long while she slept like a baby. She woke up in the morning with a feeling of so much peace in her heart. In the shower, she sang her favorite hymns and psalms. She sang Psalms Twenty-Three, 'The Lord is my Shepherd, I shall not want', and also 'O Lord my God, when I am in awesome wonder'. When she finished bathing and stepped out of the shower, everyone who had heard had a smile on their face, including those she knew could barely speak or even understand English. Music - the power of praise and worship. Especially when singing comes from the depths of the heart, full of true meaning, it is so powerful that it can move even most hardened of hearts. Deborah had been so grief-stricken that she had completely forgotten that her Jesus lived.

John ushered her into the interview room in the morning as promised the previous evening, and before she could take a seat he told her that her first interview had been slightly out of the usual, and that was why he had asked for extra time. She didn't know what to say to this, so she just kept quiet. He asked her if she had slept well, and she told him that for the first time in a long while she had slept like a child. His face lit up with a smile. "Very well then, let's see what today holds for us!" he said.

Deborah's mother finally paid a visit to the village. The moment she set eyes on her daughter she could tell that she had been well looked after. Then she apologized and explained that she had left home as soon as she had received the letter from Grandpa telling her about the birth of her child. But Deborah could see the guilt on her face, the guilt of not being able to explain why she had not come even once to see her in the village despite her promise. This was the first time they had seen each other after Deborah had been in the village for ten months, and the occasion was uncomfortable and different. She remembered that the last time she had seen her mother, she had been in a lot of pain, and had felt abandoned as a child. She simply could not understand why she had been bundled up and taken to the village.

But now, a full ten months later, she had matured and undergone a complete transformation, and her mother knew that. The tough lessons of life had changed her from a child to an adult in less than a year. Her mother could see that change, and so she was very calm and collected, and now that they were together again, she made it clear that she fully understood. She immediately started to tell Deborah about the plans she and her father had for the future. Deborah was told she was to return to school the following month, and would still be at Our Lady of All Saints. But she was not to tell anyone that she had had a child, as that was not the story they had told the school about her absence. Finally, her mother was going to adopt her little boy as her own son. She was happy that she would be returning to school, but she was not sure about returning to Our Lady of All Saints because to her horrible ordeal. However she had no choice. She could not fault her parents for the decision, as they really seemed to want the best for her future.

The principal of her school was a woman, and that was one of the reasons why she loved Seat of all saints - it was uncommon to see or hear of a female principal. In her society, the post of principal was considered a position of power. In Deborah's homeland, when power is mentioned one automatically thinks of men, so it was very inspiring for other girls and especially her to see a woman in control of the school, and it made her aspire to greater things in life.

She returned to school at the end of March 1992, when the school year was already half way through, but because of her previous performance, the principal allowed her to re-join her peer group in the second form. She was a little taken aback at the decision that she should go into the second form as she had been off school for half the school year. But the principal spoke to her personally and reassured her that with determination and hard work everything was possible. She concluded by telling her that she was a wise little girl and she would do just fine. So Deborah left her office feeling greatly encouraged, and determined to be the best.

The rest of her school years at Seat of all Saints went smoothly, with no further incident. She encountered no questioning of where she had been or what sort of illness had befallen her. Her parents had dealt well with the issue of her absence. Nevertheless, her day-to-day experience at the school was unbearable. She over-reacted to every sound and any footsteps approaching her. She was unable to stay in the classrooms or go anywhere alone. She was very frightened at times, and even imagined people coming to get her. Crying was a common occurrence – sometimes she wept all night, only stopping to promise herself that when she came of age she would definitely avenge the crime that had befallen her. Such thoughts gave her some consolation, even though she had no idea how she was going to take her revenge. At times the way she acted was so odd that her friends thought she was disturbed or even crazy; others felt her behavior was to draw attention to herself. But how could they have known that Deborah had been so brutally violated? She was one of their classmates in the beautiful school that they all loved and trusted, in which they felt secure and protected, an institution they know as one of the best schools in the nation! Deborah sometimes wondered if her parents' decision for her to return to Seat of all Saints would have been different if they had known the true story of her pregnancy. Finally she was persuaded to believe she was protected by the grace of God all through her school years, however whenever she thought of her earlier experienced, it stopped her heart beating for a while.

CHAPTER 7

Awaiting Trial

At 19, with 3 A 'Levels and a five-year-old son, Deborah decided university study was not the way forward for her. She started a small business with her university tuition money and a year down the line she had a convenience store in her home town. Her parents felt pleased at her business acumen, but were not happy as they still believed the only way from poverty to riches was through education, and a university degree would have been a good start.

With more money in her hands, Deborah could now participate in other activities. She decided to join the Southern Cameroon National Congress (SCNC), a socio-political group that favored the complete secession of the southern British Cameroon from French Cameroon via peaceful negotiations. The group also campaigned for the well-being of the British Cameroonians and for the rights of women, so she was devoted. She also saw joining the SCNC as the best avenue for expressing her grievances and avenging her past. She strongly believed that many other girls were suffering as victims of rape incidents. She knew that still more would suffer, but if she and other women helped the SCNC to succeed in its aims, they could be sure their young girls would be safe. Better still, if southern Cameroon was able to secede from French Cameroon, then many of their young girls would not be molested and raped by the armed forces and police ever again. By the age of 20 she was a fully registered member of Southern Cameroon National Congress with frontline duties such as organising peaceful demonstrations and conferences. The government definitely saw the group as a threat, and orders were given for the arrest and torture of its members. Trying and dangerous as it was to take up frontline duties like that, Deborah needed to feel involved; it was also a form of personal revenge for her. For five years, as a member of the SCNC, she suffered inhuman torture, detention without charge and further rape at the hands of the police and the armed forces.

Her last arrest was the longest and most brutal period of incarceration, and she decided she did not want to die and she could not bear it any more. She was detained for nine months while awaiting trial, but without any charge, and she was subjected to dehumanizing treatment. The warders would pile onto her, rip off her clothes and whip her breasts with a rubber belt, and she would cry until she could cry no more. The food was disgusting, and sometimes there was no food at all. She was not allowed regular showers, and sometimes it was so bad that she was disgusted by her own stench. She was convinced that she was going to die awaiting trial. This time she was detained for much longer, and the torture was unbearable, but she also had bad news when she had been detained for three months: the chairman of the group had been murdered by government officials, and he was usually the only one who could negotiate members' release. She tried to draw strength from the fact that she had a son who did not know his father's identity, and she had to stay alive for him no matter what, but it offered scant comfort. All through her ordeal she prayed for a miracle.

Her boyfriend, Smith, visited her at least once a month - he was such an inspiration to her. They first met when she had just joined the SCNC at their first annual conference. He told her that he was attracted to her because of her passion for the cause of the SCNC, her positive attitude and her strong personality. She loved him so much because he was such a gentleman and had a lot of respect for woman.

Then Smith resigned from the party. That was three years before her last arrest, and it was because of the increased violence inflicted on members by the police. He urged her to do same, but she refused and instead felt her boyfriend was a coward for resigning. He had asked her to give up her role as the party organizing secretary so that they could get married and start a family, but she declined. It was not that she did not love him enough, but she could not accept that he had abandoned the cause they all so strongly supported because of crude threats from the government. But then she did see why he had left the party. Lord, he must have had foresight, for he understood that more suffering would befall the members. Smith had a favourite saying, and he would use it whenever she was headstrong and wanted things *her* way: "Debbie, you know, you can never affect changes from the grave."

They had had different reasons for joining the party. Deborah had personal grievances, so even if she had known there was danger ahead she would still have hesitated to resign without any further reason. Now, whenever he visited her as she was awaiting trial, he kept urging her to think of leaving the party if she managed once again to get out of detention alive. He said this because there was rampant killing of the party's top officials and nobody knew what would happen next. Members who had abandoned the party recently were still being targeted by the police. So abandoning the cause now did not guarantee freedom and safety. Even if you left the party now, you might still be a target for life unless you left the country and went into exile.

Smith would sometimes talk at length about Deborah's son, and remind her that the little boy deserved to have a mother to guide him through life. He also urged her to be reasonable and not be selfish, as there was so much to life and family. His visits made her long for all the good things life had to offer and think how it hurt to be in such a godforsaken place awaiting trial. But she always looked forward to his visits; he was like a lifeline between her family and herself, passing on all the information he thought it necessary for her to know.

Night was the most unbearable time in the cell, with everything dark and scary. The inmates were left alone to face their thoughts. The mattresses were so thin you could feel the springs on the bed piercing through your skin, but that was really not as much of a torment as the thought of not being free and not being able to see your loved ones. She missed her son, siblings and parents so badly. She had regular news through Smith that they were doing fine, but that was not enough. She also missed the love she shared with Smith. She imagined his gentle kisses and caresses, and she closed her eyes in pain at the thought of the love and peace they shared, the lovely surprises and gifts he showered on her; and she cried in despair as she wondered if things would ever be the same again.

CHAPTER 8

Fugitives

Every now and then, the inmates were taken out to a warden's farm to work as a form of punishment. Deborah had no idea that the male prisoners were planning to overpower the warders on one of these trips so that some of the lucky ones amongst them would be able to escape. On that momentous day Deborah was one of the prisoners who had no idea of what was going to take place. The cell unit they were detained in had not been in trouble, nor had any of the convicts escaped from it for a long time, and so only two warders were assigned to guard them at the farm. On their way to the farm, the male convicts were on their best behavior, and telling jokes. They argued about who was the strongest and who would do the most work, and the warders themselves were relaxed and spoke only occasionally, just to calm the male detainees so that they would not get excited and noisy.

As they arrived at the farm, and the warders were still planning how work would be shared for the day, two convicts attacked each of the wardens, hitting them on the head with a stick and instantly knocking them out. John asked if this was when Deborah had killed the man, and she looked at him sternly and said, "I told you *I* killed a man, and I did not say a group of prisoners killed a man." He muttered an apology.

The convicts had to strike early so that when they were expected back in the jail at dusk, they would have had plenty of time to get away, and even to cross the border into a neighboring country. At first Deborah was confused, and did not know what to do. She had not planned to run away from detention, but the opportunity had presented itself - and it might be her only opportunity. Her heart was racing, and questions that she could not answer were rushing through her mind. What if she got caught? She thought of the torments they would put her through. She had to pull herself together and think fast. Within a twinkle of an eye, the other detainees had disappeared into the nearby bushes, and there was no one left but the two warders lying on the ground. Everything was happening so fast.

Instinctively she started running and crying at the same time. She was overwhelmed by feelings she could not identify. After running for a while she realized that she might be going nowhere. She had no idea what direction she was running in, so she stopped and held her breath for a while .She told herself that she had to be calm and work out what to do quickly. She needed to think of a way out of the bushes by remembering how they had found their way onto the farm. There was not a moment to lose, otherwise she might not be free for too long.

They were not allowed cash in the prison, but if on visiting days a family member could sneak money in without the authorities seeing it, then it was a good thing. The money could be of great use to them some day if they managed to hide it properly. She was thankful that she had had the presence of mind to hide five thousand Cameroon Francs in her private part. She always had there for security and in case there was trouble and she needed to buy her way out.

Finally she managed to remember the route they had taken to the farm, so without any hesitation she took to her heels. She ran for a while, and then started walking as fast as she could. Somehow she must have lost her way, as after a while she arrived at a solitary house sitting almost in the middle of nowhere. She approached silently and looked around carefully. There seemed to be nobody in the house, as it was so quiet that even the sounds of the dry leaves under her feet startled her. There were some men's clothes on a line outside, so she quickly took off her prison uniform and slid into a pair of trousers and a shirt. The clothes were very ill-fitting, and on her they must have looked as though they were on a clothes hanger, but she did not let that bother her. Any clothes would have been much better than the prison uniform as all she needed was something to hide the fact that she was a prisoner. Without any further thoughts she hurried out of the compound and into the bushes again.

It took her a good one and a half hours to get to a paved road. She could hardly make out where she was. When she stopped the very first car that came her way and told the driver where she was heading to, he gave her the fare for her journey, and it was only then that she realized she had made most of her journey on foot. At the main bus station, no one recognized her, and she was grateful for that. Her oversized clothing also did not seem to attract attention. The bus station was as busy as ever, and everyone seemed to be in a hurry. The bus drivers and the loading boys were shouting and jostling each other in their attempt to get passengers – just as they always did. Deborah was thankful to find a bus that needed just one more passenger before it was full and could leave, so she hopped in.

The normality of what was happening at the bus station also indicated that their escape had not yet come to light. And nobody on the bus said anything about it, so she felt more relaxed. It was comforting for her to know that no one except the prisoners who had escaped were aware of what had happened. It took a good hour and a half before she arrived at the place where Smith worked. He owned a very large bakery in the country's economic capital, but joined in all the work just like the staff, so that few people would have guessed that he was the owner. He spent most of the time at the bakery checkout collecting cash, as staff were always stealing his money.

When she reached Smith's place, she stood by the side door near the main entrance for a while. He was very busy with customers. She watched him carefully so that she would see if he looked up and she would be able to beckon him to come outside, but he was too busy to look away from what he was doing. She was getting very nervous as she knew she might be running out of time. However, one of Smith's workers had seen her staring, but seemed not to recognize her as she heard him talking to Smith and referring to her as 'a crazy woman'. He told Smith that Deborah had been standing by the doorway and staring at him for more than 15 minutes.

But then Smith did look up slowly, and when his gaze met hers, he immediately stood up as if he truly thought she was an insane woman and was about to shoo her away. Then as he approached the door, the looks in his eyes told her he knew who she was. He pulled her gently into his arms and held her tight, and then took her into his office. At first he was confused, because he knew she was not due for release, or certainly not any time soon. After she had told him what had happened that day, he stood up, stared at his wristwatch for a while and said, "you do not have much time!" He told her she had to go to her mother's village immediately, as it would be difficult for anyone to trace her there and recognize her. He promised to stay in the town and work something out. He gave her some more cash, and told her he would be at the village in a week's time. When she turned to leave, he pulled her back and said, "You have to leave this country – going into exile is the only thing you can do!"

Deborah reached her mother's village at nightfall, but it was a good 45 minutes before she arrived at her grandfather's home. Vehicles normally dropped passengers off at the market in the town centre, and they had to make their way between the hills to get to Grandpa's compound. As she walked along the bush path, the sweet smell of roasted cocoyam and fried vegetables lingered in the air, reminding her that the evening meal was being prepared or eaten. The chirping of the crickets and the night lark's song were a warning, reminding her to hasten her strides as it was now past the time for any sensible person to be out in the dark, no matter what the reason might be. The familiar lights from the table lamps shone through the holes of the thatch walls and illuminated the path, and she was grateful for that.

As she approached Grandpa's compound, all the bitter-sweet memories came back. There was also light coming from Grandpa's hut. She wondered who was living there now - Grandpa had died in May, 1992, the year she gave birth to her son. Hearing how close she was to her grandfather, the principal of the school had granted her permission to attend his funeral. She had been terribly shaken by his passing away, and the memories threatened to bring back tears, but she managed to fight them back. This was no time for crying: she needed to focus on her present situation. Deborah knew deep in her heart that she needed to keep a clear head. If she were to stay free and alive, then she could not allow herself to be overcome by emotion or memories.

She first made her way to the hut of Grandpa's last wife, Sarah. Sarah was surprised to see her, and even more shocked when she examined her closely and saw the state she was in. She was absolutely emaciated, she cried. Then she joked about the men's clothing she was wearing, and said Deborah looked like a farmer's wife who had run away from her husband's house in a hurry, and they both laughed. When she asked what she was doing there, Deborah told her how she missed the village, and missed her, too. She said that after all these years she wondered how they were faring, and that was why she had felt she had to stop by. Sarah told her it was nice of her to come, but also shook her head as if to say that she was disturbed by her story. She looked at Deborah again and saw that she must be very tired and hungry, telling her that she would prepare a bath for her and something to eat, and that they would chat in the morning. Deborah just nodded, as she was too tired to say yes.

Deborah slept until after midday the next day and was only woken by the sound of Sarah pacing up and down in her room. Sarah told her she was worried that she had slept for too long. She said that she needed a change of clothing, and offered to lend her some. But Deborah declined, as she had enough money to get herself new clothes at the local market. Sarah reminded her that the local markets did not stay open late like the township markets. The stall-keepers usually started packing up their goods by late afternoon, and as it was already past 1 p.m, they would have to make haste if they wanted to buy nice clothes, or indeed any clothes at all.

Deborah and Sarah took the little bush path leading to the main road. It was a walk that they were very familiar with, something they both loved and cherished from the time Deborah had come to live in the village. It was always an opportunity for the two of them to gossip about anything out of the ordinary in the compound and the village. Some of Grandpa's older sons from his first and second wives had been under the impression that they might still have had a chance with Deborah in spite her being pregnant. Other men in the village had promised her marriage after the birth of her child if she would allow them have sex with her. Sometimes, if the men did not want to use a direct expression, they would say, 'if you allow us to visit your Jerusalem'.

Whenever Deborah told her what the men wanted from her, Sarah would cry out in horror. She maintained that it was taboo for a pregnant woman to sleep around with men that men were all liars, and that most of them only think of their own satisfaction. She said jokingly that if a skirt was put on a wooden carving, most if not all of the men in the village would thrust their manhood into it before realizing that it was not a living object. Sarah also said it was appalling for a pregnant woman to sleep around, and if a woman was caught doing so for whatever reason she would be ostracized by her kinsmen. All this was said in a tone of deep concern: She did not know that Deborah was all too familiar with the base motives of men, and that she was currently in the village as a result of a wicked soldier using her for his sport. Nor was she aware that Deborah's father in particular did not want anything to do with her as he considered her a wayward child. Sometimes she wondered if Sarah would show her the same care and love if she told her she was pregnant not of her own will, but because some man had treated her as a plaything. But Deborah knew better than to let any amount of love and care from Sarah force her secret out of her.

As Grandpa's youngest wife, Sarah was the envy of all the family. One could tell clearly that she was Grandpa's favourite wife, and Grandpa made no attempt to keep it secret. Her name was the first thing Grandpa would say when he got up in the morning, and he consulted her before embarking on any trip or project. The very name

Sarah name seemed to be a sweet melody to him, and in return Sarah showed him respect and reverence. Even though Grandpa was much older than Sarah, her love for him seemed to make him look younger, and when he was with her he behaved like a young boy. Sometimes when Grandpa was with his other wives, the older ones would team up against her or tell lies about her just to steal some of the love he felt for her.

Sarah was pleased when Deborah returned to the village. She felt she had a confidante to whom she could talk about all the things that bothered her, and the only time she could talk to her without any fear of someone listening was on their way to the market. Today, however, their walk to the market was different, for there were no exciting stories about the boys and men in the village or wives' conspiracies, and no ignorant questions about childbirth; instead it was full of uncertainties and unanswered questions about what the future held for Deborah.

Smith got to the village a week after Deborah had arrived. He had kept his word, and she was very excited to see him. She hugged and kissed him, and was all over him like a child. Smith went round the compound so he could say hello to everyone. When they returned to Sarah's hut, he pulled her closer and started explaining the events that were taking place in the towns and cities as a result of the escape. He told her that all the major newspapers and radio stations were talking about it, and broadcasting photos of the escapees, too. He said they were lucky that the two warders the male prisoners had knocked down had not died, and were now recovering steadily at the hospital, for otherwise the search for them would have become an international affair. He also told her that the police had visited his business to enquire if he had seen her. They had

61

questioned all the staff at the bakery, and it was lucky that none of them had any idea that she had been there. None of them could have imagined it was Deborah in the oversized men's clothes she had been wearing. He said his movements were being watched closely, and that is why he was disguised as an old man. His disguise was really good, and he did look like an elderly man with white hair and a beard. She was glad he was being very vigilant and cautious as one can never underestimate the police. He told her that a reward of 5 million CFA had been promised to anyone who could give information about any of the convicts' hiding places.

As he was telling Deborah all this, she was shivering like a bird that has been soaked by a heavy downpour. She was worried that the size of the reward was so tempting. It was the kind of money that most villagers could not dream of ever having or even setting their eyes on, so if anybody - including members of Grandpa's family – was aware she was worth so much, they would not hesitate to reveal her hiding place. In her anxiety, she grabbed Smith and held him tight. She was truly frightened, too terrified to respond to Smith's pleas to tell him what was going on in her head. She held him so tight that he himself was frightened.

When Deborah was calm enough to speak again, she asked Smith to tell her what her fate might be if the police caught up with her. She had an idea of what might befall her, but she was confused. She wanted to know what she could do to save herself, or whether it was too late to think of safety. She was certain that she would not be able to survive another week in the prison or bear further torture in the hands of the police. Smith said he could not say for certain what would happen to her, but promised her that he was doing his best, and making arrangements so that if possible she would be able to escape to another country.

How might that be possible, she asked him, if there were police officers everywhere, with an added police presence on every major road in the country. She started crying quietly.

Smith put his finger across her lips and gently kissed the tears rolling down her cheek. Then he saw more tears on her lips and kissed them away slowly. She wanted to say sorry for crying and tell him how frustrated she was, but when she opened her mouth to speak the words would not come out. He looked into her eyes and said, "I love you so much, Deborah." Still she could not find the words she wanted to say. The torture and immense humiliation she had suffered in detention for almost a year was still very fresh in her mind. She had seen a more devilish side of men - men who had been given trusted positions in society to protect people, but who blatantly abused this power and got away scot-free.

Her relationship with Smith had taught her that men are not all the same, that some are honorable and can really offer a shoulder to cry on. The thought of his kindness and gentleness towards her made her very happy, and there was a tiny smile at the side of her mouth, although she was not looking at him. He said again, "I really do love you, Debbie." She thought to herself that that was something she could never forget. It was Smith who had completely changed her perception of men. He had convinced her that some men are born to love and cherish a woman. She raised her head, looked at him and whispered slowly that she loved him, too, and that she had survived the terrible ordeal of detention only because of the hope that someday she would be free again and would be able to share her love with him. He pulled her closer to him and placed his hands around her; she could feel his heart beating as she placed her head gently on his chest. He gently kissed her forehead, her cheek her lips. Their emotions began to flow, and they pressed closer, savouring the delicious sensation. He began kissing every single part of her body, and the rhythm of his breath felt as though he was writing a love song. His fingers reached for the first few buttons of her blouse and caressed her breast, and she groaned with passion. Her fingers fumbled with his pants, and soon their bodies moved against each other as they felt their breath and every fibre of their being filled with hunger for more. The next morning she woke with a warm kiss pressed to her forehead and their legs tangled together, and she made a promise to herself that she would rather die than go back into detention. More than ever, she was now determined to be totally free.

CHAPTER 9

The Great Escape

Fearing for their lives and the torture that might face them, Deborah's parents sold her business and the family house and moved to an entirely new town. Smith knew all about this as he was the one who informed her about what her parents had done, and he said they had promised to bury the proceeds of the sale somewhere under the ground so they would be safe. That was a wise move, as when one is on the run or on a most wanted list you cannot afford to put your money in a bank or financial institution because the government would not simply freeze it: they would steal it all and leave you penniless.

Strangely, Deborah's parents had now become her stronghold, perhaps because when people get older they become wiser and probably forget the things that hurt the most. Who would have thought her parents would make an effort to safeguard her money and watch her back? Now that she was grown up and had more experience, she was tempted to forgive - drawn to forgive her mother and father for the way they had treated her when she was violated and became pregnant. Deborah tried hard to convince herself that because parents protect, educate and offer guidance to their children, they may feel disappointed when bad things happen to them and take the frustration out on the child.

But what if it was not the child's fault, as in her case? She could have died in the village during childbirth, given that she was so very young and had had no proper medical attention. It scared her now to think that if she had stayed in the coma just a little longer she would have been buried alive in accordance with tradition. It was so distressing to think that the people she looked up to had abandoned her to her fate because of their pride and social position. Deborah's parents had been afraid that friends and family would laugh at them and call them names. But who made man the judge of mankind?

She hoped that someday she would be able to find the strength to tell her parents the true story of what actually befell her that fateful day at Seat of all Saint College. Or someday that she would muster the courage to say, "Mama and Papa, I was not a bad girl as you thought, because I was raped, violated, destroyed. And that was why, after you mistreated me and tortured me I was still unable to show you the father of my child, as I truly did not know who he was". She wanted to be able to say he was a completely alien father. He was very tall, like a man mountain, and his skin was as dark as night. He was very strong, too, and at barely thirteen years of age your little girl had no strength to fight him off, and she believed that as a man her father would understand. If only she could also tell her mother that he smelled bad, that his body odour was like the smell of stale cassava *fufu* .His teeth were the colour of red earth and after he had finished with her she had fainted. Deborah knew that as a woman her mother would understand. And she wanted to be able to explain to her parents that they should not consider her passion for the SCNC as a crazy whim, because she was driven by all the bad things that she had experienced as a child. She would have loved to see the look on their faces when she told them the whole story. It might console her to hear them say, "We are sorry, Daughter, we wish we had showed you some love."

Smith succeeded in arranging for her to flee the country. He was introduced to a man who could organise such things. The man demanded to see Deborah's most recent photo before he was able to make the travelling arrangements. When Smith presented the photo to him, he said that Deborah had a strong resemblance to his wife. All Deborah had to do was get a nose ring, as the woman in the passport was wearing one. He told Smith quite openly that he did this sort of thing for a living, and it was all about the money; if they had money, in three days she would be out of the country. Smith accepted the deal, and paid part of the costs on behalf of Deborah. The two men agreed payments would be completed once they were able to sneak her away from the village and closer to the international airport in Douala. Deborah thought that was a wise move, because there was a possibility that she might be caught before she arrived in Douala.

Her journey to Douala was dreadful. She had the identity card of a Muslim woman who was Smith's friend. He told her that when he was trying to work out how to get Deborah out of the village, the idea of stealing the friend's ID card had come to mind. He paid her a surprise visit at her shop in the market, and while she was busy serving customers and chatting away, he knocked her purse onto the floor and apologised, but as he was picking it up he stole the ID card. Deborah mocked him jokingly, telling him that she never knew he had such skills, and he replied that 'desperate times call for drastic measures'.

In less than half an hour the captain announced that they would be descending to land at the Murtala Muhammed airport at Lagos, Nigeria. There was another announcement shortly after the first to advise that everyone should remain seated and keep their seat belt fastened as in less than an hour they would take off again. Deborah fell asleep; she felt very tired, but she also slept also out of fear, weariness and uncertainty. When she woke up the plane was in the clouds, for she had not realised that it had taken off. That was good, as the previous take-off at the Douala International Airport had been very frightening for her. She could not really tell what was happening, and didn't even know where they were going to. Jude, the man who had made all the arrangements, had only said to her that he was taking her somewhere safe, somewhere beyond the reach of the evil hands of the government.

Yes, she was very excited about the thought of running away, running away to some far-away, unknown place where she would find peace. Now, as she sat in the plane and looked at Jude from the corner of her eye, she was unsure. The excitement she had felt was now giving way to terror, as she did know her final destination. She turned her head in his direction and stared at him, but he was sleeping. He did not look at peace at all. She thought about waking him up to ask where he was taking her, but she was unable to move because of her fear. As she watched him, he started snoring, his mouth wide open. She did not like the sight of him at all. At that moment he looked completely untrustworthy, like someone who is not afraid of committing crimes. There were strange scars on his face, three on each cheek, like a punishment to tell the world that he had betrayed somebody. Deborah turned away quickly and started to wonder if she had now got into even more trouble. That could be something she might never be able to escape from. In her confusion, she looked across the aisle and her eyes fell on the male passenger sitting there. He gave her a warm smile, and she smiled back.

She must have drifted off for a while, as she felt a gentle tap from the air hostess on her shoulder, who asked her if she wanted meat or fish. She was still trying to work out what the air hostess wanted when Jude interjected and said, "Fish - give her fish," and she nodded. Jude ate like a glutton; he kept calling for more food and drinks. He reminded Deborah of a sow they had called Doris. This was just what Doris would do, and she was even known to starve her piglets. But Jude was eating in a way that might have starved a whole nation. She was so embarrassed at the way he was eating that could not chew a mouthful of her own food. The sound coming from his mouth was like children clapping their hands in a playground. Crumbs were sprayed everywhere, and she thought even the passengers at the back must have heard the noise he made. With his head still buried in his tray of food, he grumbled into the bread he was eating that the flight was so expensive that people had to get their money's worth in any way they saw fit. She covered her face with her hands in disgust, but he was too busy with his food to notice. She asked herself how anyone could be married to Jude, even for a day. She prayed to God in his infinite mercy to rescue her.

Jude looked at his watch, then at her, and told her that in less than four hours they would be in London. He was silent for a while before saying, "do not forget we are husband and wife." He gave her a piece of paper and asked her to re-write and then slowly recite all the information he had given her about his wife. She did as told, and when he was satisfied he took back the paper and tore it into shreds. To show he was satisfied he attempted tried to smile at her, but it was the weirdest smile she had ever seen in her entire life. Deborah reminded herself that she had to be careful with Jude, for if something as simple as a smile could threaten to deform his face even further, then he must indeed be an unusual person. He told her he needed to be sure she had internalised the information, or they would get into trouble when they arrived in London. So she was going to London, she said to herself, and she started to feel a little happier.

As Deborah examined the passport Jude had given her, she saw that she bore an amazing resemblance to his wife. They could have passed for sisters, except that his wife looked much more mature.

John Biggs gave a big sigh of relief, and felt grateful he had been born and raised in England. He closed the book he had been writing in, and said he would present everything Deborah had told him in the best possible way so that the Home Office would be able to make a decision. He stood up to leave, but suddenly remembered she had not told him how she had killed the man. Deborah asked if she really had to tell him, and he said he would only be able to decide after he had heard the story, but that it could be relevant. She felt that John was sincere, and now that she had told him so many intimate secrets, she thought there could be no harm in revealing one last incident.

She had not planned what happened, and had certainly not intended to kill anyone. But it was all so fast, and she was left in a state of shock herself. One night a warden had come to her cell and he'd taken her to the back of his office. She hated the smell coming from his breath and from his body. The first time she had tried to resist, and he punched her so hard she thought she was going to black out. She told herself to be calm. After he had had his way with her and she had returned to her cell, she made a promise to herself that henceforth no man would lay a hand on her against her will. She was tired of being treated like trash, and she knew she would be better off dead than being used as a plaything. She started planning ways of protecting and defending herself against these serial rapists who called themselves warders. Her first idea was to get a sharp object to give anyone a fatal wound if they came too close for comfort.

Although she had not planned to take a life, that fateful evening when she heard the warders talking about the 'sudden demise' of another warder in the corridor near her cell, she knew immediately that she had killed someone. She was full of relief, but on the other hand scared they might realise what had happened. Astonished, John asked her how she had done it. She had never thought it would be so simple, and had no idea someone would die from their own pleasure that night.

The warden who had punched her the previous night had come again to claim another pound of flesh. This time he was drunk, but not so drunk that he could not find Deborah's cell. He came straight to the door and opened it, commanding her to come out. Remembering his heavy fist the night before, she obeyed without realising that he was drunk. As they approached the back of his office, she saw that he was stumbling and not walking straight. In his befuddled state he called her a prostitute, told her that she belonged to him, and said that he could kill her without anybody asking a single question. He went on talking, and she smelled his filthy breath as he said, "today I want to enjoy myself," and "I want maximum pleasure from you." Deborah stood motionless, looking at him. While he was still talking and cursing he managed to pull his trousers halfway down, and told her to help him take them off for him. She did as she was told, and then he wanted her to take off his boxer shorts. They smelled of stale urine, but she was left with no option.

He spread his body flat on the cold floor, and through the alcohol fumes he said, "Suck this - or else I will kill you." When Deborah looked at what he was referring to, she saw

71

he was holding his penis in his hands. He told her to suck nice and slowly, and fearing for her life she knelt down and held his penis in her hands gently, so that he closed his eyes in anticipation of the pleasure she was going to give him. She pulled it upward, exposing his testicles. She knew that the only weapon she had were her own teeth, and began thinking about the best point of attack. She realised that the scrotum was softer, and she would be able to sever the testicles with a single bite. She positioned her mouth carefully, and told him that he should lie still if he wanted to experience the ultimate pleasure.

To Deborah it was the easiest and most satisfying thing she had ever done. She slipped back to her cell as quickly as he had forced her to leave it. He had made the other warders afraid of her, telling them all that she was a witch and warning them to stay away from her. Now he died with her name on his lips, but the devil prevented him from telling anyone what she had done. She had killed a man with a single bite to the most sensitive part of his body.

John looked at her with an amazed expression, and said, "You are bad!" but all Deborah did was shrug her shoulders. He said jokingly that if ever it ever got into the news or the papers that someone had been killed by a single bite to that part of their body, then he would know exactly who had done it and tell the police. They both laughed, and she told him that it would only happen if anyone forced her beyond her limit and had his crotch near her teeth. He reassured her that he would not write this part of her story down, as it was of no relevance to the matter in hand. He then asked if he could tell his wife, as she might be very interested to hear how she had dealt with the man, and Deborah said, "Permission granted!"

Three days after this, John returned with the terrible news that her application for asylum had been refused. He could see the fear in her eyes, and reassured her that she had nothing to worry about. He said that she had a very solid case to be allowed to remain in England as a refugee on humanitarian grounds. It was against Article 8 of the United Nations Human Rights Convention for England to return an individual to a country when their life was in danger. He also said that the Home Office official who was dealing with her case had clearly misunderstood the facts. The documentation informing her of the refusal contained several claims which had no basis in fact, including references to associations and organisations she had never been a member of. This made her feel a little better, but she was not truly sure of what to believe.

She had the right to appeal within seven working days, and John had already launched the appeal on her behalf.

CHAPTER 10

Luton

Misery needs company, and this was true for the guy Deborah encounter in Luton. She had a week's break from life in Oakington when she was sent to a guest house in Luton. She was told that the officials needed to decide which of the asylum camps she should go to, so staying in Luton for a week would give them time to find one she could be moved to. She was advised that her application to become a refugee in Britain was being fast-tracked, so the most time she could spend at the reception center would have been eight days. Within the eight days she would have been properly assessed, so even if the officials could not find a camp for her immediately, she had to be hosted somewhere in the interim.

The place she was sent to was an old building, and small, too - it could barely pass for a guest house. There was scaffolding outside, which indicated that renovation work was taking place. The room was just enough for her, with a small TV in one corner, a tiny school-sized bed and a stool to sit on. The lady who worked there was very polite, and told Deborah there were no set times for meals as in the small kitchen one would always find something to eat and there was always plenty. The lady understood her business very well: she knew there would be people who had no sense of time, and so there was no point in drafting meal schedules. Everyone at the guest house looked tired and shabby. Deborah did not recall meeting any of them at the reception centre, but it looked as though they might be in need of some form of help and support. Most of them were white, but they spoke different languages. She could hear them talking in the corridors and sometimes when they met at the breakfast table.

She was frightened out of her wits one evening as she came out of the kitchen after dinner. It was just after six, and being winter season, everything was dark but for the lights from the tiny lamps in the hallway. As she opened the door from the kitchen, she saw one of those white skinned men standing by the stairway that led to her room. At first she thought he was waiting for a friend, but as she went past him he whispered something. If she had heard him right, the words were 'I love you'. She thought he must be talking with someone, even though there was no one about. She looked round to see if there was anybody else there in the tiny, partly lit corridor, and he pointed at her and said, "You, yes you - I want to fuck you".

Deborah let out a mighty scream, and within seconds the woman who owned the guest house was dashing towards them. But the white man had already disappeared and was nowhere to be seen. She was shaking with fear and was immediately sick; all the dinner she had eaten came rushing out of her system. The woman took her back to her room and helped her clean off the splashes of vomit on her clothes. Deborah looked terrible, and the woman was worried about her and asked what had happened. She said it was just an attack of nerves, and explained it was something which was happening more frequently because of bad experiences in her past. The woman reassured her that the guest house was very safe, and that they had never had this sort of incident before.

When she left, Deborah bolted the door but was unable to sleep as she kept thinking the man could come back and break down the door while she was asleep. She was becoming increasingly fearful of men, especially those that wander around alone. Their intentions are always evil. She reminded herself that she could always attack them in the same way as she had dealt with the warder, but worried that white skinned men might be tougher targets. That tactic could not guarantee success every time, and she knew that.

Her shock at what had happened did not wear off for a long time. One thing was for sure: the white man must have seen her as a plaything, something to use for his pleasure that evening. The incident would come back to mind when she least expected it, and she would let out a scream. Men! Men! Men! Why did some women seem to be cursed with them? Surely God in all his glory could not have created men to instill in them such a casual attitude towards rape and all the other brutality she had suffered at their hands. Why have they chosen woman as their instrument of gratification and the victim for their torture? Women are to be treasured and cherished by men. Could there be a world without men? Deborah had promised herself that for as long as she lived no man would lay hands on her unless she wanted it.

On her departure from Oakington, she was handed some files and a card. Her friends in the asylum informed her that the card was a voucher worth ten pounds, to be used within a fortnight. Deborah assumed the papers she had been given explained what the card was for, but she didn't bother to read them as she was already fed up with paperwork, so all she knew was what her friends had said. She was aware that if you want to hide something from a fool, the best place is inside a book - fools will never read it. Deborah already had a plastic bag full of official papers, all bearing her signature. She complained that the amount of paperwork she had to carry around was more than half a suitcase, and that it was definitely a thousand times more than all the papers she had come across before arriving in the United Kingdom. She wondered to herself why the people of Britain seemed unable just to say something and leave it at that. She was convinced that the need for signatures on every other document was a symptom of the mistrust which existed in the country. Usually, when an official asks, 'do you understand?' you'd better start looking for a pen, as the next sentence is, 'sign here.' Deborah had put her signature on so many documents without having any idea of what they meant, but thanks to God none of them had yet returned to haunt her.

CHAPTER 11

Lincoln

For Deborah, the city of Lincoln was a city of great importance and left many memories. She settled down quite easily in Lincoln. A woman from Zimbabwe befriended her as soon as she arrived at the asylum centre. She gave her a brief history of everyone in the building. Deborah felt this was very important, as she did not want to step on anyone's toes. But she spoke very little of herself, as saying too much could always lead one into trouble. And to tell the truth, the history lesson she had had from the Zimbabwean woman kept her out of trouble.

Lincoln smaller than other cities, but it was full of rich ancient history that she found fascinating. She learned that by Norman times, Lincoln was the third city in the realm in terms of prosperity, and even had its own mint for making coins. It was a beautiful city with amazing landmarks, including the must-see Lincoln Cathedral and the Castle situated at the foot of the great Lincoln Hill. She was *richly* informed that Lincoln Castle was steeped in history spanning the centuries from 60 AD right up to the present. Two years after the Battle of Hastings, William the Conqueror began building Lincoln Castle on a site which had been occupied since Roman times. Deborah was in awe when she saw the first structure at the site for the first time, the Lucy Tower motte and its bailey, to which another motte and stone walls were added early in the 12th century. She was told by the tour guide that when it was completed it dominated virtually the whole skyline, including the nearby Lincoln Cathedral. For 900 years the castle had been used as a court and a prison. Many of its prisoners were deported to Australia, and others were executed on the ramparts. She really believed that she would never meet anybody in the world who would not be left in wonder by the beauty of both the Cathedral and Castle.

The city of Lincoln might have been all new to her, but Lincolnshire was a name she did know, and she had formed a picture of it in her imagination. One of her greatest idols, the poet Alfred Lord Tennyson, was born in Lincolnshire, and she had studied his selected poems at her high school. She thought his narrative poem 'The Charge of the Light Brigade' was a masterpiece. Deborah felt it was inspiring to think that a group of soldiers should believe and obey a commander, a leader, even though they knew full well that it might lead to their ultimate end. Although the poem was an account of the battle of Balaclava during the Crimean War, she believed the message was just as relevant today. And the message was one of courage, of believing, supporting and encouraging leaders even when they blunder, for to err is human. Lord Tennyson's message should be heeded by the people of today, she felt. And it was even more important that each and every person should be able to take charge of their own destiny and existence, no matter how difficult that is. This should be the case even if it meant one had to die trying.

The city and its people were warm and friendly, and it was probably here that Deborah finally regained her sanity. She was a Roman Catholic by birth, but there was no Catholic church near West Parade, where she lived. She was not choosy about churches as she knew God is God, and He is God alone. She went to one church after another, and finally found that the Baptist Church was the one she could most easily relate to. The experience was remarkable. At the church they were all one big family, with everyone willing to help. The trouble was that

79

everybody wanted to know and understand why she was in England. Deborah felt that in a way this was a good thing. Some members of the congregation showed genuine concern for her wellbeing. However, a few people seemed to think that she had no right to be there. One could sense that in the tone of their voices when they asked what had made her come to Britain, or how long she had been living here.

Worse still, as soon as somebody had been told about Deborah's situation, they would walk up to her and ask if she was an asylum seeker.

More often than not Deborah would respond to personal questions, even if they were asked in a rather condescending way. But she cursed such people under her breath: 'May our good Lord deafen you with thunder and lightning!' before confirming that, yes, she was an asylum seeker. There was a note of challenge and defiance in this, as if to say, 'so what are you going to do about it?' And so the questioner would have nothing more to say except to acknowledge the information with an 'mmmmh', as though they had just realized that the question was very stupid, and they would turn around and walk away as swiftly as they had approached her.

She concluded that men all over the world are generally not meddlesome. They had their downsides, but that certainly did not include idle gossip. Women, on the other hand, and especially elderly women, would poke their noses into all sorts of things which were not their business. This seemed to be ingrained behavior, even though they always reaped the reward of their nosiness like an inquisitive monkey who gets a painful slap.

Deborah clearly remembered one occasion after a service

when an elderly woman asked her when she would return home to Cameroon. "Never!" she replied. The look on the woman's face was full of disapproval, as if to say 'how dare you not want to go back!' Deborah looked at her for a second and decided she had better shut this old lady up once and for all. So she moved closer and said, "It might be of interest to you to know that I am not on vacation in your beloved country but an asylum seeker. I am here because I desperately need a safe haven!" She went on to tell her that where she came from her life was in danger, and but for this she would not have left her own country. She further made it clear to the woman that when she had thought of fleeing her homeland, she had no idea that she would end up in England. But now that was here she believed it was the right place for her.

Then she immediately asked, "Do you want to know why?" Without giving her a chance to say anything, she answered her own question. She could not suppress the emotion in her voice as she recounted how Great Britain, this wonderful nation, had seized her own country, Cameroon, and occupied a third of it for almost four decades. They had brutally changed the culture, language and way of life of the people. And that was before the start of the unspeakable slave trade in the coastal areas of Cameroon, in which the United Kingdom was one of the main participants. They had bled the land dry, and when it was time to quit they abandoned the land to an unknown fate. The excuse given for this callous, unworthy behavior was that Cameroon was not ready for independence yet - it was still a 'banana nation'. They had left the nation at a crossroads, without any thought of the challenges independence would bring. Deborah shook her head in despair as she described this catalogue of inhuman behavior.

She then asked the elderly woman another question: "Who do you think was responsible for preparing Cameroon for independence?" The woman's eyes grew wider, and she had difficulty getting her words out. There was no need to respond to that, she said, as they both knew the answer. Deborah reminded her that she was in England only as a result of the negligence and uncaring attitude of the English nation. But she also made it clear that she could look the lady in the face and forgive her and her country for all the untold suffering meted out to her ancestors, the consequences she herself had suffered and which those who followed her generation would continue to suffer. So who gave her the right to get annoyed if she decided never to leave England? At these final words from Deborah, the lady turned around and slowly walked in shame as she must have been convinced by her body language to think so.

Deborah arrived in Lincoln on March 9, a day before her birthday. The caretaker of the asylum centre picked her up from the train station. The camp was a three-storey building with 25 rooms. She had to say it was far better than all of her previous residences. She had a room to herself, with a much bigger bed and more space. She was also allowed to shop and to cook her own meals. It really felt like freedom. The West Parade building was known by many inhabitants of Lincoln as the asylum centre. Well-wishers would frequently leave gifts for the asylum seekers at the main entrance of the building. She thought it showed great kindness.

Deborah had to change her solicitor. The nearest office of John Biggs' firm was in Leeds, which she was told was another huge city, although not as big as London. Given the experience she had had in London, she certainly would not want to go anywhere strange all by herself. One of the girls in the asylum centre told her about a very good immigration solicitor in town, so she made an appointment to see her.

She had really wanted John to carry on with her case. The last time they had met, when he had received a response from the Home Office, he had explained to her that he worked only in the Cambridge area. Hence if she was taken away from Cambridge, there would be a new solicitor or even an entirely new firm dealing with her case. However, he did promise her that she would not be made to tell her story again. He had carefully and clearly written down everything she had told him in a concise and appropriate form. And the promise was indeed kept, as her new solicitor never bothered to ask her to repeat any part of her story. Thinking of John Biggs again and his kind words and reassurances brought a lump in her throat. She felt terribly sad that she might never be able to see him again, for he was such a gentlemen. He had relived her terrible experience with her, and had made things much easier by sharing with her the burden of telling the terrible ordeal of the rape incident for the first time.

Deborah now realized that two years was plenty of time when you are all by yourself in a strange land. She spoke to Smith, her love, and her parents every now and again. She was very lonely. She had good reports from her parents about her son. She was very grateful to be alive. A month after arriving Lincoln, she could not bear idling around any longer. She took up a voluntary position in an office in a small village on the outskirts of Lincoln. Three months later, the company owner offered her a paid job as her asylum claim had been approved. Her employer believes in diversity and was open-minded, and within a year she had learnt a lot. She had plans for Smith and her son to join her soon in England. When she spoke to Smith, they talked about a great future together. She told him all her great stories about England: about the generosity of the people, and of how she appreciated the fairness of all the services. Her favorites stories were about the queuing system: it was so good to see people wait patiently for their turn to be served in the queue, and such a contrast to the corrupt system in Cameroon, where those who were rich or knew the right people had priority. There, the better your contacts, the quicker you got served.

One story Smith made her tell time and time again was about how she had come to know her first employer. She told him that when the idea of volunteering with the company was first mentioned to her, she had thought it would be work on a dairy farm milking cows, as the company had 'cool milk' in its name. But to her embarrassment, it turned out that the company dealt with free and subsidized milk for school children as part of a government subsidy scheme. In her ignorance, the weekend before the start date she had gone to the shops and bought Wellington boots and farmer's jeans and a jacket.

But when the man who was to introduce her formally to the company arrived to collect her he was not happy at all. He seemed disappointed, and thought she was not ready to go along with him. So he was surprised when she told him that she was really excited and looking forward to the work. At this he burst into laughter and asked her what on earth she thought she was doing all dressed up like a farmer's wife. She explained that as she would be working on a farm, then of course she would be milking cows. This time he laughed even more, and could not stop. Eventually he told her that the company dealt with administration work for kids who wanted to drink free and subsidized milk during school hours, and so she had better change

84

into a more appropriate outfit.

Each time she told this tale, Smith would let out a small giggle on the other end of the phone. He called Deborah 'Smarthie', a name he had given her two months after they met. He got the name from a cat he had, who was always racing around and getting into trouble. One day the cat had managed to jump into a fire and burn almost all its fur. He said Deborah was always trying to do too many things at the same time and forgetting she needed to take care of herself. Now she told him that she was no longer a busybody as she had been in Cameroon. Life in the United Kingdom was peaceful and organized. You could not get busier than the system allowed. If you were a civil servant, the system had mapped out a pattern for you, and you could only break free if you started to think out of the box. He felt that might be a downside, and she agreed that of course it was. But the good thing was that you could become self-employed and own your own business, just like her current employer: he was the owner of his business and Managing Director. He had set up his business all by himself.

Her new solicitor was wonderful, and what was more, she was a woman. Her name was Elizabeth France, but she said Deborah should call her Liz. After their first appointment she wrote to request her case file from John's firm. John Biggs had reacted to everything Deborah told him with anger and aggression, horrified that anyone should be subjected to such suffering, and Liz also felt that no one should have such torture inflicted on them. She firmly reassured Deborah that she should rejoice, as she had come to the end of her suffering. Deborah could feel her sincerity, and she believed every word she said. Liz was a professional and a very warm person, and she was always a breath of fresh air when they met. She told her

85

repeatedly that everything would be alright, that it was only a matter of time. She was glad she had had these two solicitors as they had been the key to a new and better life. They had relieved her of a burden she had carried for so long. It was as if they had put her on an operating table and delivered her of a long overdue baby. Now she understood that life was a series of frequent changes. Some changes are welcome, while others range from inconvenience to catastrophe. Deborah had had to cross so many bridges in her life, and the seasons had all been equally hard. There was a lot of truth in the saying that 'falling down is part of life but getting back up is living.'

CHAPTER 12

Out of Sight

Nevertheless, life still had one mighty blow to deal Deborah, and she thought she might never recover from it.

Smith was starting to act strangely in their phone conversations. He did not sound as excited as before, and would not laugh as much. He made too many excuses – he was busy with work and had lots of other family projects. When she called at night, he was too tired to speak. She tried to rouse his interest with the story of the farm and the milking. But he would complain he had no time to listen, or - even worse - he would listen with little enthusiasm. She pleaded desperately for him to tell her what the matter was, but he said he was fine. She loved Smith very much; he was the centre of almost every thought and action she took. She wanted a family with him. He was caring towards her, and had all the qualities and attributes she wanted in a man.

In addition to owning a business, Smith had learnt a bit of computer technology, and she loved the way he played with the photos she sent to him. A printed design he had made from one of her photos hung above her bed post, and she looked at it every night before she went to bed. He had chosen photos of the two of them and combined them into one, in which they hovered half-naked in space. He had arranged it so that there was a heap of their clothes on the bed, and they were playing with them. Deborah felt he had a very artistic mind and was creative as well. She loved that about him. He had said he missed her so much, and she believed him.

She was heart-broken when she received an email from him with just a photo of a baby and no message. But the meaning was clear to her – there was really nothing to write. It all made sense now: his lack of enthusiasm over the last few months was all because of his new woman. She felt that this had happened because they were miles apart from each other, and had no idea when they would see each other again. She was completely shattered and she almost cried her life away. She felt she would have gone insane if she had not been able to cry so much. She did nothing for a whole week, and for the first time she felt insecure again. She felt bitter and jealous of the mother of his child. She should have been the one to bear him a child - not some strange woman! Smith was a good man and she envied the new woman in his life. She never doubted that he would make her happy. She could not stop looking at the photo of the baby he had emailed. The baby was a girl, and she looked exactly like Smith. He was not the kind of person who did anything without thinking about it very carefully. She knew definitely that he had moved on.

What she did finally may have seemed extreme, but she had to do it for her own wellbeing - so her heart would not split in two. First she took a pair of scissors and carefully cut the picture he had made of them together into separate parts. She went to the Lincoln library and made a copy of the part with Smith on it. She glued this to a sheet of fine paper, and at the bottom wrote in bold letters:
"IN LOVING MEMORY OF MBA SMITH
ALPHA 2001 OMEGA 2005"
She put Smith's picture in a small wooden coffin she had made herself and buried it in a little hole. And the second one she put just where the previous photo had been. He had to die so that she could live again.

Deborah lives on………..